DreamScape

*Creating New Realities to
Transform and Heal Your Life*

∾

Nicholas E. Heyneman, Ph.D.

*A Fireside Book
Published by Simon & Schuster*

FIRESIDE
Rockefeller Center
1230 Avenue of the Americas
New York, NY 10020

FIRESIDE and colophon are registered trademarks
of Simon & Schuster Inc.

Designed by Paula R. Szafranski

Manufactured in the United States of America

1   3   5   7   9   10   8   6   4   2

Library of Congress Cataloging-in-Publication Data
Heyneman, Nicholas E.
DreamScape : creating new realities to transform and heal your
life / Nicholas E. Heyneman.
p.   cm.
"A Fireside book."
Includes bibliographical references and index.
1. Dream interpretation.   2. Dreams.   3. Symbolism.   4. Dream
interpretation—Software.   I. DreamScape (Computer file).
II. Title.
BF1091.H46   1996
154.6'3–dc20   96-24949
CIP

ISBN 0-684-81917-1

ACKNOWLEDGMENTS

My deepest gratitude to all my students, clients, and friends who shared their dreams with me. You have been my greatest teachers. My heartfelt thanks to Julie Castiglia, Kathy Messano, and above all, to Cathie Heyneman, without whom *DreamScape* would never have become a reality.

For Sasha and Jonah,
who fill my dreams of joy.

TABLE OF CONTENTS

PREFACE

This book is about creating a new personal reality through the power of dreams. It is about living the life of your choosing by learning to recognize what is important and what is not, by understanding and feeling your emotions accurately and honestly, and by empowering yourself to achieve your goals. It is about becoming the person you wish to be.

DreamScape represents the beginning of a new era in dream analysis—an approach to dreamwork made possible only within the last generation with the coming of age of computer technology applied to human potential and human problems. This new method of dream understanding enables each of us privately to explore and decode the mysterious and very personal language of the unconscious mind in a way never before done. We now have at our fingertips the interactive advice of dream experts spanning time and cultures synthesized into a simple personal system.

DreamScape is a book and software, a virtual reality tool kit for decoding the mysterious language of dreams. Its new method forces us to think about our dreams, and therefore ourselves, in a completely new way. It rejects the tired metaphor that dreams are visual stories and instead boldly asserts that *dreams are real,* powerful emotional experiences communicated to awareness from the unconscious mind.

Dreams are powerful because they connect us to every bit of who we are. They peer into the mind, from our deepest, darkest secrets and desires to our rational selves. They examine our bodies—diagnosing health and disease states that our doctors may not be aware of for years. They inhabit our soul, feel the strength of our spirit and our yearnings, see our past, and even connect us to the past of all life. Dreams sense our future and our place in the universe.

Dreams transform themselves to be whatever we expect them to be. *Dreaming is a mirror of waking reality, reflecting needs, desires, expectations, beliefs.* If we're concerned with our health, then our dreams will be somatic, telling us about our body. If we're struggling psychologically, then dreaming will focus on our mind. Our dreams will oblige no matter what our concern, be it for spiritual guidance, companionship, problem solving, prosperity, or emotional or physical healing. And if we believe that dreams are nonsense, then nonsense is exactly what we will find.

DreamScape releases the power of dreaming for those of us who have only barely thought about our dreams. It is sophisticated yet easy to use and understand, and very personal, like private time with a dream expert—each interpretation is unique, each collection of symbols special and different. It will teach you about your dreams' unique and very special language and guide you to discover the meaning of those puzzling, exhilarating, fascinating, alarming, and even terrifying dreams.

The *DreamScape* Method

DreamScape is a comprehensive method that walks you through the entire process of dreaming, from dream recall to interpretation. Each step of the way, *DreamScape* explores your most personal inner attitudes, abilities, feelings, beliefs. It was designed to tap the rich psychological, physical, and spiritual vein that dreaming exposes, making connections between symbols and the events of everyday life.

The *DreamScape* method is a book and computer software. The book is self-contained—you can benefit from this book even if you choose not to use the software. It provides all the information you need to understand dreaming, dream interpretation, and the power of dreams in everyday life.

The software contains two programs, one that analyzes your dreams for you and another that is a personal electronic dream journal. Record your dreams in the journal and use its sophisticated search capabilities to find any symbol in any dream, to compare your dreams, or to make notes about them. Then use the *DreamScape* program for a very personal interactive analysis of any dream. The software was designed for ease of use—it requires no previous computer experience.

The *DreamScape* method is a *dynamic expert system*—a knowledge base compiled from contemporary science as well as from the traditions and lore of our long dream history. Its interpretive material is based on years of research into many different dream interpretation methods. Represented are contemporary psychology; Eastern and Middle Eastern philosophy; Egyptian, Roman, and Greek mythologies; Native American traditions; biblical parables; and New Age beliefs. *DreamScape* synthesizes these philosophies into a single, comprehensive, yet easily understandable system. It's as if a Jungian psychologist, a Middle Eastern cleric, a Native American medicine man, a New Age mystic, and a Buddhist monk were together, discussing your dream. Each has a unique perspective, but somehow all seem effortlessly to dovetail to a common truth—something for you then to take, consider, ponder.

I think you'll find that the *DreamScape* method is new, different, more powerful, more comprehensive, cutting edge. It's not just another dream book or another dream dictionary; it's much more: it is about creating new realities to transform and heal your life.

The Power of Dreams

Through dreams we are given a great gift. We spend a third of our lives touching an energy with the power to transform us to whatever we choose.

We spend this time unencumbered by physical distractions and open our minds to greater self-understanding. We can become aware of our unique strengths, creative abilities, and personal resources, discover how to protect and vitalize our health, and focus our thinking so keenly that decisions seem automatic. We can learn to heighten our awareness to a level that makes it seem possible to read the future. We can recognize the best path for personal achievement and prosperity, how to revitalize our families and communities, and how to seek healthy and lasting relationships. We can even nourish the soul and choose a path of contentment, peace, and security.

The third of our lives that this wisdom is available to us is the time that we spend in dreams.

Unfortunately we haven't been taught the truth about our dreams. No one takes us aside to open our eyes to this realm of wisdom, so most of us assume that dreams are visual images—fanciful, amusing, absurd, frightening, sometimes even terrifying stories that we watch as we sleep. Even Webster's got it wrong. *Dream* is defined as

A sequence of images passing through a sleeping person's mind.

A much better definition would be

Awareness of unconscious feelings and impressions.

The dictionary definition states what most of us take for granted: Dreams are pictures, moving randomly through our sleeping minds. Yes, dreams are visual, but they are also much more. In fact, our improved definition makes no mention of visual images at all or that these images are noticed in any particular sequence.

The essence of a dream, its meaning, its power, is contained in the feelings and impressions that it leaves with us.

Sometimes these feelings and impressions are expressed through symbolism, other times through pure dream emotions. The *DreamScape* method decodes these feelings, stripping away distracting images and exposing the true meaning embedded within a dream.

How Do I Interpret the Symbols and Emotions in My Dreams?

> I was standing in the middle of a great war. There were machine guns firing and bombs exploding, there was billowing black smoke everywhere. I could see the bodies of soldiers being torn apart; they were being killed all around me. . . .

This should have been a terrifying dream, but it wasn't. The images were violent, bloody, and threatening, yet John, the dreamer, felt no fear, no sense of the danger that would be reflexive in waking life.

If you heard only John's dream but not his reaction, then the dream's meaning would be lost. Like a movie without sound, the pictures are telling only part of the story. It's John's *feelings* that are the key to understanding—the calm he experienced in the midst of the lurid imagery. John might just as easily have strolled through a crime scene or a street brawl, got caught in a *Star Wars* battle or by a volcano erupting; it would have made little difference, as the pictures in his dream are of little importance. They are fantasy, yet John's dream was *real* because the feelings he experienced were real.

> My dreams create a personal reality when I accept that the emotions I feel in a dream are real.

If a dream is what we feel and *not* what we see, then its reality becomes clear. These emotions are pure—feelings that usually lie just beneath the level of conscious awareness. They are real because they are what we *truly* feel, not what we believe we *should* feel.

In John's dream, a calm walk through a battlefield represents the peace he feels with himself in the face of great changes occurring in his life. His dream reinforced the difficult decisions he was making as sound and necessary, and for John this reassurance was welcome, as he had always struggled with decisions, worrying that he might make a wrong choice. But as he listened to this and other dreams, the choices he needed to make became clear, almost automatic, filling him with a sense of confidence.

It's tempting to lose ourselves in a dream's images or be distracted by some amusing absurdity, but it's not the visual quality of a dream that gives it meaning; it's the feelings, the impressions that it leaves—it's how we *experience* it. Dream images are what's called *epiphenomenal*—meaning that while they may be interesting, they're not important. Dream pictures can come from anywhere—a late night movie, a news story, a triggered memory, a fantasy, something that happened to you the day before. But dream feelings come from only one place—the unconscious mind. And the unconscious mind connects us to parts of ourselves and the universe that conscious awareness is blind to.

It's only natural to believe that dreams are like a mental movie. That's because when we think back on a dream, we make sense of it using everyday logic and reasoning, and we're inclined to put it into the most familiar framework, the most obvious analogy that we can —and that's a movie.

The illusion that dreams are visual stories with characters and plots seems convincing, but it's false. There are several important differences between movies and dreams.

Characteristics of movies:
- Linear, a beginning-to-end time frame
- Defined characters and sets
- Structured plot and fixed scenes

Characteristics of dreams:
- Nonlinear time frame, in the present
- Feelings and impression
- Freeform, without plot
- Dynamic, flowing scenes

This may seem obvious, but stories need to be listened to from beginning to end; a movie run backward wouldn't make much sense. Even coming in in the middle of a film is confusing since you miss what happened earlier, such as character and plot development. You can't *step into the middle* of a dream. It's not linear; it doesn't run start to finish like a movie. Any part of a dream is important, as long as you are aware of what you're feeling.

My dreams create a personal reality when I accept that dreams are impressions and feelings and not stories.

Also, if you think about it, the visual quality of a dream is never quite the same as a film. In a sense, dream reception is fuzzy, with one scene quickly and sometimes erratically cutting to the next. Some dreamers do report ultravivid images, but this is not as common as we tend to think; perhaps just 10 percent report such images, usually the same people whose daydreams and fantasies are so lifelike that they can blur reality. Those who journal excessively pictorial dreams have usually learned to do so, mostly under the mistaken belief that this is what a dream is supposed to be.

Dreams also differ from stories in that the latter have defined characters and situations, fixed and written into a script. The plot is structured and unchanging. Dreams, on the other hand, are dynamic, as dream elements flow freely without restriction. Their emotional impressions sometimes percolate quietly and other times erupt violently into consciousness.

So don't be confused by a long parade of images or a twisting plot; emotional symbolism is usually simple. And a dream's feelings don't necessarily have to be linked by a seemingly rational plot in order to be understood or for its power to be felt.

> My dreams create a personal reality when I accept that
> dreams are never scripted but are experiences that ebb and
> flow as pure liquid emotion.

Dreams often seem bewildering—nonsense that in any other context might be considered a breach of sanity. More often than not they don't fit logic as we know it; yet they're a place where nothing surprises us, where we're willing to suspend disbelief using the simple and, if you think about it, utterly circular reasoning that the experience was *just a dream.*

I once had a client who repeatedly dreamed that his head lived on the body of an animal—sometimes he was a turtle, or a monkey, or a lizard. Naturally these images seemed quite absurd to him—no one, of course, has the head of a man and the body of an animal. But, as would any of us, my client accepted his dream's absurdity; after all, *it's just a dream*—and since we've all dreamed with similar breaches of logic, this seems a perfectly understandable and acceptable explanation.

But while the images may seem bizarre, the dream is not. That's because it's the feelings and impressions within the dream that give it power. *If we feel a dream, we can always translate its symbolism into meaning.* This is what makes each of our dreams unique; they are as intimate and personal as our own feelings.

Once we accept the reality of our dreams, its symbolism comes alive and its power can be felt. The *DreamScape* method releases the power of dreams by guiding you in exploring your own unique and very personal dream reality. You'll find that symbolism is in the eye of the beholder—what's profound and moving for me may hold no special significance for you.

While dream symbolism is as unique as each personality, the first step in interpreting dreams is recognizing that its reality lies within its feelings and impressions, not its pictures. This means fighting the natural inclination to make judgments and associations, to piece together a plot, to record the experience, to analyze, rate, and compare, to chart progress.

Finding an inner emotional reality is actively choosing to simply feel what comes, letting all else take care of itself. It's closing your eyes and adopting an attitude of less reason and more feeling.

For human beings, naturally selected through millions of years of evolution to create a rational experience, creating an inner emotional reality seems alien. The *DreamScape* method simplifies this process and thereby releases the power of dreams by forcing us to acknowledge a dream's feelings and interpreting its symbols in the context of the impressions that they leave.

What Are My Dreams Made Of?

While many dreams seem bewildering, they are actually quite simple, containing only two elements: *symbols* and *emotions*. Dream *symbols* are pictures, actions, and abstract concepts, while *dream emotions* are the feelings and impressions associated with the dream. Together these symbols and emotions are called *aspects*.

When you are interpreting a dream, it's helpful to divide its aspects into two components—*primary and secondary aspects*.

The Primary Aspect

The *primary aspect* is that symbol or emotion that you, as dreamer, somehow find most compelling. It may be an image, color, action, abstract concept, sensory impression, or vague or distinct feeling. It may be the most obvious feature or somewhat obscure. *But it's the emotional epicenter of the dream—the piece that feels most important.* For the sake of simplicity, there is only one primary aspect for each analysis. For example, consider the following dream:

> I was being chased by a huge, salivating dog, and while running, I noticed a small oak tree in the distance. . . .

You could choose as your primary aspect yourself, the menacing dog, its saliva, the implied fear, the chase, or the small tree—but choose only one, whichever feels right.

Always consider your primary aspect before deciding on anything else about the dream. It may be a quick and obvious choice, a feeling or impression that stands out clearly, but it may also be difficult to choose, in some instances, at best an intuitive guess. If your analysis doesn't make sense, rethink it and then do it again, trying a different primary aspect.

Secondary Aspects

A dream may also contain various *secondary aspects*—symbols or emotions that you intuitively feel contribute to the dream's message but are less prominent than the primary aspect. Secondary aspects are optional—some dreams will contain them, others will not. But it's best to limit the number you choose, as haphazardly loading an analysis with symbolism overly complicates and dulls the clarity of your interpretation.

Take, for example, the dream I just mentioned. *Dog* may seem the most likely candidate for primary aspect, and most people would automatically choose this symbol—*but feel the reality of your dream.* You may, instead, choose *chase* or *fear* or *salivating* as your primary aspect. Any of these aspects may also be secondary, and you may even decide that the dream's most obvious symbol—the image of the dog itself—is *not* needed in the analysis.

Dream Fragments

If you are having trouble identifying the primary and secondary aspects of a longer dream, the dream can always be divided into smaller bits, or what are called *dream fragments*. This makes a dream's impressions more manageable, its feelings more apparent, and forces us to recognize that it's not a story. Use your intuition to create these fragments, guided simply by what *feels* right. For example, here is a dream and its possible dissection:

> Climbing down a hillside, I saw three wolves eating a carcass. I tried to hide behind a rock, but it kept disappearing, leaving me exposed. . . .

Here are four possible dream fragments for this dream:

1. Climbing down a hill
2. Three wolves eating flesh
3. A disappearing rock
4. Exposure

It is usually best to analyze each separately, with its own set of primary and secondary aspects. You may decide that only one of the four dream fragments is really important; feelings associated with being exposed, for instance, may be the crucial message in the dream. Once you begin to feel your dreams, the choice becomes clearer.

Finally, leave your rational self behind for the moment and accept that the power of your dream is contained within its *feelings*. As a practical method, concentrate on the *verbs* in your dream, the actions, and deemphasize nouns and objects. Ask yourself, from moment to moment, what you *feel*.

My dreams create a personal reality when I stop trying to make rational sense of them and instead just experience them.

How Can I Use My Dreams to Create New Realities?

Dreaming empowers us to create new realities to transform and heal our lives. Our dreams do so by teaching us what is important and what is not, by helping us feel our emotions accurately and honestly, and by empowering us with the strength and skills necessary to achieve our goals. Our dreams help us to create a life of our choosing.

Fortunately nothing is easier than learning from our dreams. *As soon as we begin to focus on a dream's emotional significance, we begin to create a personal reality.* It's automatic, it's not a matter of effort or even choice. This shouldn't surprise us, as most learning during our waking hours is automatic. To use a simple analogy, most of us have learned the hard way not to shake a soda can before opening it.

My dreams create a personal reality when I discover the emotional reality within a dream.

Learning from dreams is also automatic. We benefit just as soon as we begin to attend to our dreams, and we learn in many different ways. At times dreams teach specific lessons, such as how to solve problems, face a new situation, or achieve a creative goal. Sometimes dreams guide us, charting a course through business matters or relationships. Dreams often reassure us and open our minds to spiritual guidance. Most frequently, however, dreams tell us about ourselves—what we feel, what we believe, who we are. *As soon as we begin to accept the emotional reality of dreams, no matter how often we remember our dreams, we begin to see these effects.*

Dreams are like a mirror, reflecting whatever is important to us at the time—the needs, desires, expectations, and beliefs that concern us. They morph to create whatever reality we expect. They are always egocentric, that is, selfish as a small child is selfish—concerned about us and no one else. And they tell us whatever we *need* to hear, although not necessarily what we *want* to hear.

If you're consciously or unconsciously concerned with your health, your dreams will certainly be somatic, telling you about the condition of your body. If you're depressed, anxious, or struggling with an emotional problem, then dreaming will focus on your mind and your emotional suffering. If you're looking for answers to a troubling relationship, your dreams will search with you. Problem solving, spiritual guidance, companionship, whatever concerns you is the stuff of dreams. And if you believe that dreams are nonsense, then nonsense is exactly what you will find.

My dreams create a personal reality when I realize that dreams morph to reflect my needs, desires, expectations, and beliefs.

How Do I Use the **DreamScape** *Method?*

The *DreamScape* method is powerful yet easy to use. As you go through the book you'll see that because dreams reflect the needs and desires of the dreamer, most dreams fall into one of six categories that form the book's chapters: *self-understanding, health and healing, relationships, prosperity, spirituality, and prophecy.*

Each chapter contains two main sections. The first describes the chapter's category of dreams, teaches you how to recognize them, how to increase their frequency and potency, and how to harness these dreams to transform your personal reality.

The second section in each chapter presents the six fundamental symbols for each category. While these dreams may take many forms, these six themes underlie many hundreds of dream aspects identified using factor analytic methods, sophisticated statistical techniques that classify dream symbolism into thematic categories. These are the emotional themes that constitute dream reality and give symbolism its power. Use them as a guide, recognizing that each dream is unique and personal.

You may also use these chapter sections as a dream dictionary. First, find the dream symbol or emotion (aspect) that is most prominent in your dream in the alphabetical aspect index at the back of this book. You'll find the theme that your symbol is associated with as well as the page number(s) where this theme is described. Because dream symbolism is different for each of us, many aspects are discussed in more than one chapter. For instance, images of *clouds* are associated with symbols of *faith* as well as *opportunity*, so there are entries for this aspect in both the Soul and Prosperity chapters. Choose whichever sections are most appropriate given the feelings and impressions of your specific dream.

The *DreamScape* software is very easy to use, with complete, step-by-step instructions included within the program as well as in appendix 2 of this book.

It doesn't really matter what you do as long as you do something. *Even if you remember your dreams only on occasion, you will benefit.* By the way, if you would like some strategies for improving dream recall, see appendix 1. So don't be scared off by thinking that you must record and analyze your dreams religiously or they are of no value—any dreamwork is useful.

Continue on now, and *create your own personal reality* through the power of dreams.

CHAPTER ONE

Dreaming for Self-Understanding

⁓ Dreams of self-understanding, those that reveal our emotional and psychological well-being, are by far the most common we experience. This shouldn't come as a surprise, as we seem to live in an age of psychological turmoil—confronted almost daily with stress, depression, troubled relationships, and financial worries of one sort or another. In fact, dreams of self-understanding are so common that only recently have we begun to recognize the *eclectic* nature of dreams, that they mirror health and spirituality, for instance, as well as our emotional state.

What Is the Psychological Power of My Dreams?

Dreams of self-understanding can be exceedingly powerful, at times unnerving. That's because we are protected from painful feelings in waking reality with defenses that we're not even aware are operating. Dreaming cuts through these defenses, exposing our most personal and basic needs, fears, and desires—feelings that are rarely experienced consciously, but boil just below the surface of awareness.

A scientist and writer came to me with this dream, one that he has experienced repeatedly since he was a young boy:

> In my dream I'm a boy dressed as a man wearing a huge, oversize coat that hangs off me. I'm being chased by gangsters. Although I'm terrified and running as fast as I can, I can't shake them because I keep tripping over my coat. . . .

Edward finds his dream emotionally jarring and especially puzzling because of the overwhelming sense of inferiority and helplessness that it always leaves with him. He describes the feeling as a physical sensation—as if his solar plexus, the region just above the stomach, is being ripped apart, exposing a bottomless cavern of fear. It is sometimes several hours into the next day before he feels himself again. This seems so out of place given someone as successful and apparently sure of himself as Edward. How could he possibly be feeling so insecure?

Edward's dream *does* reflect genuine feelings of insecurity and inferiority—feelings buried for years beneath the grandiosity of his position, achievements, and awards. For all his accomplishments Edward is a *psychological impostor;* he has never been the confident person the rest of us assume him to be. Because of early childhood abuse he was never able to form a healthy, positive self-image. Instead he hides behind a huge, protective, bigger-than-life coat: first of good son, then of top-of-his-class student, and now of renowned scientist. Sadly, his achievements are unconsciously driven by fear, not desire.

But behind this grand mask is a small, frightened child—and this child is constantly on the run in his dreams, desperately afraid of being exposed. Edward's dream helped convince him to seek out psychotherapy to heal the wounds of the small abused child within him.

No social position or influence, no achievements, no awards, no amount of prestige or money, can fool the unconscious mind. Fame, prominence, possessions, prestige, won't make us someone we're not —and dreams always tell us who we *really* are. Dreams are honest and unprejudiced and feel no need to conform to any social pressure. They never *put on a front* to impress someone because that *someone* would be us. As Dr. Carl Jung, one of the world's most brilliant dream experts, once said, *"Dreams are impartial, spontaneous, and show us the unvarnished truth."*

> My dreams create a reality of self-understanding by revealing truths about myself spontaneously and impartially.

Because dreams can be blunt and because we're not used to this kind of brutal honesty in our waking lives, dreams can seem frightening or alarming. But dreams are telling us about our normal human drives, motivations, fears, aspirations, and feelings. There's nothing unhealthy, abnormal, or obscene about our dreams. When a dream scares you, it's only because you haven't grasped its meaning. If a dream embarrasses you, it's because you're looking at it from the wrong perspective.

> My dreams create a reality of self-understanding when I accept that there's nothing unhealthy, abnormal, or obscene about my dreams.

What Is My Persona?

All of us wear a mask that Jung called the *persona*. It's what we let others see of us in our various social roles—student, employee, spouse, parent, church member, and so forth.

Our persona is the character we assume in daily life—it's usually what our friends know us to be—and it is, of course, shaped by our desire to be looked upon favorably.

Think of your persona as roughly the difference between the way you act in public and the way you are when alone. If you were to imagine yourself in a social setting, meeting someone whom you're attracted to for the first time, and then describe how you act, you're likely describing your persona.

But what do we see when we look at *ourselves?* If we neglect the person behind the mask, if our mask never comes off, then we begin to believe that the persona *is* ourselves. Our true self gets lost—like an actor who can't distinguish a role from reality.

Persona and dream feelings are very different. That's because dream feelings are genuine; they have no need for a persona. Without hesitation they tell us about *who we really are* and *what we really feel.* While dream feelings are honest and fearless, persona feelings are an illusion, usually covering fear:

Dream feelings:
  • Honest, truthful, and impartial
  • Spontaneous
  • Fearless

Persona feelings:
  • Illusory, just a perception
  • Expedient and opportune
  • Fearful

Look for the frequency of these dream symbols to gauge how important your *persona* is for you:

  • Clothing, particularly if it is extravagant
  • External signs of recognition such as awards or prizes
  • Frequent dreams of public settings
  • Theatrical performances

My dreams create a reality of self-understanding when I accept that they reveal my true feelings.

What Are the Effects of Repressed Feelings?

Sadly, many of us are not taught to understand and express our emotions but instead learn to repress, ignore, and deny what is most natural and human. While humans naturally experience the entire spectrum of emotions, from anger and hate to love and joy, we often suppress those feelings that, at the moment, don't fit our persona. We hide behind a *cognitive* veneer, but it's not thinking and intellect that set us apart from other species, it's our ability to feel. *Even the mightiest intellect is puny in the face of unconscious emotional forces.*

However, if suppressed long enough, we become unaware of our *true* feelings and conscious only of those emotions that we believe we *should* feel. But getting in touch with these feelings isn't always easy. They can be elusive and easy to ignore, partly because we don't always want to feel them and partly because they don't fit our persona.

Fortunately dreaming allows us to get reacquainted with our emotional lives. Dream emotions are easy to feel, understand, and put into proper context because they are bare, undisguised. For instance, *dream frustration,* a common emotional theme, almost always reflects waking frustration. The same holds for nearly all human emotions: joy, happiness, love, fear, anger, sorrow, and loneliness are symbolized in dreams with pure fidelity.

Have you ever blown up at what you later realize was a trivial problem—one that clearly didn't warrant the reaction you experienced? *Chances are the fuel for this anger is repressed feelings that have never been released from your unconscious.* You may be convinced that the anger you feel is in the present, and it does feel that way, but it's not. If you think about it, you'll probably notice that these episodes tend to occur when you're tired—that's because you have less energy to repress, and repression requires a good deal of psychic energy.

Repressed feelings are powerful and can fuel our emotional reactions to present events. Remember that dream feelings always come from the unconscious mind, and the unconscious has a long memory. It remembers the feelings and impressions that we experienced as children, even infants, and that we repress and carry with us all of our lives.

True emotions emerge powerfully, sometimes uncontrollably, in dreams. That's why you may find yourself angry, even violent, in a dream when otherwise you can't easily express these feelings.

My dreams create a reality of self-understanding by calling my attention to emotional reactions that are strong and disproportionate to the cause.

Bill is an example; he lives two lives. He is a physically small, plain man, painfully awkward, and difficult to describe because every descriptor seems to be average. He desperately avoids social gatherings, and if he can't, he gets lost in the group. Bill has no real friends —only acquaintances, mostly co-workers. Those who know him at all characterize him as quiet, easy to get along with, uncomplaining. The cruel-hearted office joke is that if there's work to be done that *nobody* wants, "There's always Bill!" Here is his dream:

> There's a strong muscle-bound man, a Rambo type, with machine guns in both arms and bullet belts strapped like an X across his bare chest. He storms through the office door and begins firing madly, shooting everywhere—ripping apart people, desks, chairs, walls. He just keeps shooting and shooting until I wake up—usually drenched in sweat, my fists clenched, and a fire in the pit of my stomach that feels as if I want to kill someone, anyone, everyone. . . .

As you might guess, Bill's unconscious is screaming for change. Like a Hollywood stereotype, he rebels violently against what he sees as the injustice and oppression of everyday life. His dream acts out this rage, taking its bloody revenge on those he cannot face assertively while awake.

It may not surprise you to hear that Bill *enjoys* his dream. He sleeps a lot, hoping to relive it—a potent antidote to the profound sense of inferiority he struggles with every minute he is awake. It is, of course, more than that—it's a signal of psychological need, a call for emotional change.

How Do I Understand My Dreams in the Context of Waking Life?

Dreams never occur in a vacuum—they're always triggered by some feeling or event, usually something that has happened recently. Sometimes it's easy to identify this trigger, but not always. Even if you don't know exactly where the symbols originate, you can usually guess at the dream's context once the emotional reality of the dream becomes clear.

Ask yourself what might be occurring in your waking life that may have precipitated *how you're feeling* in this dream. Remember, dream feelings are always honest, but because waking feelings are not, what you find may seem surprising.

My dreams create a reality of self-understanding by consistently and accurately revealing my feelings, keeping me emotionally honest.

The Six Symbols of Self-Understanding

- Control
- Criticism
- Emotion
- Loss
- Self-esteem
- Vulnerability

Symbols of Control

These are dreams of *personal* control, the need deep within all of us to believe that we and not others or random circumstances influence the direction our lives take. It is the opposite of *helplessness*, feeling out of control or with no sense of control at all.

Control, even in unavoidably noxious situations, lessens our pain. Psychological experiments with laboratory animals demonstrate that when the animal can control unpleasant or painful events, they are better adjusted than those poor creatures who cannot.

Lucid Dreaming

We can create a reality of self-understanding by learning to *control* our dreams. Dream control can occur when, in a dream, we become aware of the fact that we are dreaming. This awareness is known as *lucid dreaming,* and it enables us to change portions of a dream as we sleep in order to create a more desirable outcome. This may seem impossible, but it can be accomplished with practice. For example:

> I was inside a huge spaceship, hundreds of feet tall, working on the top docking clamp, when suddenly my support broke and I began to fall some twenty or thirty stories. Immediately and automatically, I altered my dream so that I wouldn't crash to the bottom, by depressurizing the spaceship so that I became weightless and began to float safely. . . .

In this dream, through lucid dreaming, falling to a certain death was transformed to floating safely.

Lucid dreaming takes considerable practice but is a powerful tool in creating a reality of self-understanding. That's because it is our *sense* of control, not actual control, that's important. By influencing the outcome of our dreams, we begin to feel a greater sense of mastery over challenging waking situations—even events where, in reality, we have little or no control.

The practical problem with lucid dreaming is that learning to induce these dreams sometimes takes years of practice. And for reasons unknown, lucid dreaming seems to come easily for some people and is almost impossible for others. Nevertheless it's worth trying. Follow these four simple steps:

1. Whenever you wake up from a dream, stay in bed, visualize yourself becoming lucid back in your dream, and say to yourself, The next time I'm dreaming, I wish to become aware that I am dreaming.
2. At bedtime concentrate on the kind of dream you wish to experience and what you would like to produce in this dream.
3. Provide the suggestion to yourself as you fall asleep that you desire a lucid dream. Use an affirmation such as

I am free to be aware of being in my dreams.
I allow myself to become aware that I am dreaming.

Tonight I seek a lucid dream.
I am able to become aware while I dream.

4. The following morning, note and mentally reinforce yourself for any awareness, no matter how brief, that you experience in a dream. Tell yourself, Good job, I am able to increase my awareness while I dream.

Letting Go of Control

Dreams of control emerge when we feel that we're being overly controlled. Most of us experience dreams of this sort on occasion, presumably because we all feel pressured and controlled at times, and out of frustration we want stubbornly to dig in our heels to get our way.

However, *control is a paradox*—sometimes the only way to gain control is to lose it. Track your dreams and notice if you're repeatedly experiencing dreams of control that suggest it's time to let go:

♦ Dreams where you are convinced you are right
♦ Dreams of isolation or separateness
♦ Dreams when no one is listening—even if you're shouting
♦ Aggressive dreams where someone is victimized

Letting go of control is like *choosing your battles*. We don't always get our way, even when we're convinced that our way is right. And we don't always have control—there are things in life that, for all our desire, we cannot change: born an endomorph, one will never become an ectomorph. Complain, rant and rave as we like, certain situations are simply unchangeable, and accepting this reality is, paradoxically, a means of gaining control.

My dreams create a reality of self-understanding when I acknowledge that letting go of control is sometimes for the best.

Symbols of Criticism

This section could also be called *symbols of self-criticism* because these dreams emerge when we are being excessively faultfinding with ourselves. Dreams of criticism are about getting in touch with our critical side—the part of us that so easily blames when things go wrong. It compares us unmercifully with the *ideal*—and, of course, finds us wanting. It is our *superego,* an unrelenting perfectionist, criticizing us for even the smallest mistake.

Most of us can punish ourselves as no one else can, but much of this self-criticism is unwarranted. Most self-critical statements are simply not true:

- I can't do anything right.
- I'll never get it.
- Everyone would be better off without me.
- I'm no good.

These *negative self-statements* may feel real when we're depressed, but if you evaluate each statement objectively, you will see that they're always falsehoods. Dreams of criticism inform you when you are being unreasonably and excessively faultfinding with yourself.

Experiencing these dream symbols repeatedly usually suggests excessive self-criticism:

- Any symbol or feeling of criticism or personal verbal attack
- Painful biting or stinging
- Blame or accusations
- Ridicule, sarcasm, or harassment

If you choose, seek out the counsel of a trusted friend to help sort out your feelings. First disarm your critic by recognizing it and then replace the blame with *positive self-talk;* just as negative self-statements are disparaging, positive ones are empowering:

- I believe in myself.
- I can achieve my goals.

- ◆ I am free to progress at my own rate.
- ◆ I can love myself.

My dreams create a reality of self-understanding by providing an objective perspective on this criticism. I am honest with myself.

Symbols of Emotion

Dream emotions are the *essence* and *power* of dreams. If they seem as real as waking feelings, it's because they are real. While a dream's imagery is fickle—easily influenced by insignificant waking events, such as a late night horror movie—a dream's feelings accurately reflect your conscious and unconscious emotional state.

Dream feelings are unambiguous; interpret them as they feel and you find them among your most valuable teachers.

My dreams create a reality of self-understanding when I listen to my dream feelings.

While dream emotions span the entire range of human feeling, three seem to emerge most commonly: *anxiety, anger,* and *guilt.*

Anxiety

Anxiety is our most frequently experienced dream emotion—and probably our most common waking feeling as well. Mild anxiety can at times enhance performance, but severe anxiety always hampers progress. Fear of failure, making mistakes, embarrassment, or what others may think, all prevent us from self-exploration and growth.

Anxious feelings in a dream mean you're anxious in waking life as well. However, dream anxiety may also represent *unconscious* feelings that are blocked from awareness. *We often become aware of anxiety through dreaming before we recognize it in waking life.*

Feel your dreams and interpret the anxiety as follows:

If your dreams are consistently anxious:
- Fearful personality, insecure, worrier
- A tendency to live in a worrisome future
- Persistent irrational fears, such as hypochondria
- Symbols of pursuit or attack in a dream

If your dreams have only recently become anxious:
- Transient anxiety
- Something is currently challenging you in waking reality
- Symbols of an intruder in a dream

Anger

Dreams of anger are common and have psychological as well as physical meaning. Extremes of anger appear in dreams when we're struggling to deal effectively with our waking anger or hostility:

- *Externalize anger:*
  If we openly and indiscriminately externalize anger, we risk wreaking significant psychological and social havoc. We may distance relationships, alienate those close to us, and engender bitterness, guilt, and deep feelings of worthlessness.

- *Internalize anger:*
  If we internalize our anger, stuffing it deep enough so that we and others are unaware of its presence, we never really rid ourselves of it. It exists below the level of consciousness, churning and, over time, affecting our health.

- *Releasing anger:*
  As with all emotions, angry feelings were meant to be *experienced and released,* not necessarily acted upon and not repressed. We learn to recognize that anger, in and of itself, is not bad and is sometimes useful—*anger warns us that something is wrong.*

Anger can be useful by protecting and mobilizing us to escape or defend ourselves in times of physical danger. It tells us when boundaries are violated, when we are being pushed beyond what is appropriate. Anger informs us that we need to set limits or that we're being taken advantage of. It helps us overcome fear—it's easier to assert our needs when we feel angry. Anger protects us from other feelings that, at the moment, may be too overwhelming, too difficult to feel—helplessness, loneliness, sadness.

But to be psychologically effective and physically benign, we need to experience our anger and move on. This does not necessarily mean *venting*. Contrary to popular belief, venting anger is not always healthy, particularly when it's at someone else's expense. Once angry feelings are openly expressed, they can scar and are impossible to take back. While venting is not always healthy, *experiencing* angry feelings is—and stuffing them is physically harmful.

Guilt

Dreams of guilt reflect conscious and unconscious feelings of guilt. Life is a process of continual transformation, of options, and it's been said that not even God can change the past. But mistakes often engender guilt, a useful feeling if it tells us when we need to right a wrong. However, because of childhood conditioning, most of us feel more guilty than need be.

My dreams create a reality of self-understanding when I recognize that making mistakes is part of being human and an opportunity to learn.

To understand your dreams of guilt, look for the *frequency* of these dream symbols:

+ Dreams that are consistently guilty are a warning that your guilt is no longer reasonable but has become an emotional drain.
+ Infrequent dreams of guilt usually means healthy guilt—is there something you need to change?
+ Dreams of frustration—difficulty reaching a goal, completing a project, or reaching the end of something. Energy is being wasted on guilt.

Animal Dreams

Symbols of *animals* are sometimes dreams of emotion. Animals can be symbolic of *catharsis*—an emotional outlet allowing safe, healthy release when expressing these feelings is impossible in waking life. The frustration, anger, or aggressiveness that build up over the course of the day is safely let go.

Psychoanalysis teaches that the human psyche is divided into three fundamental parts: *id, ego,* and *superego.* Our primitive side—the id—represents the basic drives of survival, aggression, and sexual gratification that lurk deep within us all. The superego is like a perfectionistic conscience, scolding even the mildest transgression. The ego balances the two. It's thought that the human psyche is constantly at battle with itself, the primitive id pitted against the rigid superego, mediated by an often weary, struggling ego.

According to the great analyst Carl Jung, animal symbols represent basic human instincts and drives, the id. Animal dreams are common because we continually attempt to suppress the id in waking life, ignoring those needs and desires that may not be socially expressed, such as aggressive or sexual feelings. Our dreams are the *playground of the id,* and animal dreams often allow safe, appropriate expression of basic human drives.

My dreams create a reality of self-understanding by allowing me safely and appropriately to express my feelings.

The meaning of animal symbolism also varies by *species* of animal present in a dream. Wild animals often represent basic human instincts such as the drives for survival, aggressive self-protection, territory, or sexual gratification. However, game or domestic animals may symbolize introspection or fear. Did you sense any of these feelings —*introspection, fear,* or *aggressiveness?* As always, interpret these symbols within the context of the emotional tone of your dream.

Symbols of Loss

This section could also be called the *symbols of grief, sorrow, sadness, and disappointment* because it encompasses this range of feelings.

Emotional release is an important part of dreaming, and dreams of loss represent just such an expression. These dreams commonly emerge when you've experienced a waking loss—the end of a relationship, loss of a cherished object or opportunity, even personal changes. They can also occur as a result of your subconscious working through feelings left over from a *past* loss—either way this is a normal and natural process.

Grief

Dreams of loss are important because they encourage us to face our grief. While grief is hard to bear, and is one of the toughest emotions to work through, it is the most *psychologically healing* of all emotions. It cleanses our subconscious, allowing us to accept loss with sincerity and dignity and enabling us to move forward. It releases repressed feelings, so we do not remain prisoners of our emotional past.

Part of grieving is consciously facing and naming our loss. For instance, when we lose a relationship, we may lose

+ companionship, friendship, and intimacy
+ communication
+ sex
+ income and financial security
+ a lifestyle that we have become accustomed to

Consciously acknowledging these losses, naming them, facilitates the grieving process. Grieving is natural and takes time—just as physical wounds require time to heal, so do emotional wounds.

Dreams of grief *feel* grief-stricken and may include these symbols:

+ Any personal symbols of mourning or grief
+ Painful crying, weeping, moaning, or sobbing
+ Whimpering or despair

- Symbols of depression or sorrow
- Helpless misery or suffering

My dreams create a reality of self-understanding when I come to terms with my loss and, in doing so, face myself.

Sadness

Dreams of loss are also expressions of *sadness* and may represent an emotional release of psychological pain. These dreams are sometimes associated with the following life circumstances:

Feeling sad or disappointed:
- Symbolizes the situation associated with your feelings

Feeling regret:
- Alerts you to something you have done or failed to do

Feeling lonely:
- Reflects your loss of companionship
- Reflects discontentment with your present circumstances

Feeling depressed:
- Reflects these feelings of depression

Dreams of sadness create a reality of self-understanding when they alert us to the presence and severity of depression, disappointment, or loneliness and prompt us to seek out the comfort of a trusted friend or counselor.

Symbols of Self-Esteem

Self-esteem means loving yourself completely, unequivocally, and without qualification. It is putting yourself first, meeting your own needs, and respecting yourself. *Self-esteem is honestly and deeply admiring yourself without the need for conceit.*

As odd as it may seem, self-esteem is in short supply. When we were children, most of our teachers struggled with their own self-worth so were unable to teach us how to truly love ourselves. Lack of self-esteem is so pervasive, few of us recognize it as a problem—not many would say, "I don't love myself." But its symptoms are apparent—dysfunctional behavior, both as individuals and collectively as a society. These symptoms also appear in our dreams.

Loving Yourself

If you love someone, you pay attention to them, you act lovingly toward them, you are pleased to see them, you forgive their faults, and you *do* for them. You love them regardless of status, position, or money—you love them for *who* they are, not *what* they are. They are a part of the joy of your life, and when they are gone, there is great loss. *If you love yourself, all of these apply.*

You do for yourself as you would for the person you love the most. If you put off taking care of yourself, then your relationship with yourself, your self-esteem, is weakened. We must nurture ourselves as we do any relationship, but we are the easiest to neglect. *Dreams of self-esteem inform you when you are taking yourself for granted.*

When self-esteem is sagging, dreams feel overtly *self-conscious.* They may also feel

- tentative
- uncertain
- mildly fearful
- noncommittal

Dream imagery may be vivid or fuzzy but usually involves humans or animals who are

- small
- ineffective
- subordinate
- cowering

Creating a Reality of Self-Esteem

You can use your dreams to create a reality of self-esteem through *incubation*. Incubation is the process of seeding the unconscious to grow a desired outcome—in this instance to tenderly and deliberately express your love for yourself. Remember, dreams are dynamic, they respond to conscious intent as well as shape it. We can learn to exercise a great deal of control over waking reality as we become more adept at creating a powerful dream reality.

Incubating for self-esteem is a simple process. At bedtime, form an affirmation and repeat it quietly to yourself while you fall asleep. Keep your affirmations short, direct, and positive. For instance:

I love myself completely and without hesitation.
I practice self-love in my dream and waking realities.
I lovingly accept myself for who I am.

Actively incubate your dreams of self-esteem for at least a week, congratulating yourself for your effort the following mornings.

My dreams create a reality of self-understanding when I lovingly accept myself for who I am.

Symbols of Vulnerability

Dreams of emotional vulnerability frequently disclose a desire for psychological refuge. Jungian psychology teaches that we erect a barrier of self-protection called the persona, the outer appearance or mask we present to the world. It is the self we show in public, what we allow others to see, and no more.

Our persona is as essential for emotional protection as clothing is for physical cover. We sometimes *need* to suppress feelings that we are unable to handle at the moment. For example, when waking anxiety becomes emotionally paralyzing, preventing us from doing little more than barely surviving our day-to-day obligations, we swallow these feelings just to get through the next hour, day, or week.

But what if we neglect the person behind the mask or if our mask never comes off? Then we risk distancing ourselves from others; we're perceived as shallow, superficial, without depth.

Furthermore, these painful feelings still exist, lurking just below our conscious awareness. And if they are persistently suppressed to the extent that we lose awareness of them and are conscious only of those emotions we believe we *should* or *want to* feel, we create a psychological illusion. When this happens in waking life, our dream life is inundated with vulnerability. Dreaming keeps us emotionally honest.

Dreams of vulnerability may also accompany the emergence of unpleasant memories. Feelings associated with these disturbing memories can prompt a variety of dream themes, all designed to be emotionally protective, cushioning the psyche. Dreams are fluid and responsive—as memories wax and wane, dream aspects also change.

Symbols of emotional exposure often include the following:

+ Feeling exposed
+ Unpleasant or embarrassing nakedness
+ Recurrent dreams of clothing
+ External signs of recognition—awards, praise—
  that feel hollow
+ Recurrent dreams of public settings
+ Recurrent dreams of theatrical performances

My dreams create a reality of self-understanding when I accept that emotional security comes from finding the right balance of self-protection and candor.

Dreams of vulnerability also emerge when we waste energy concealing feelings that we don't want others to see. Although this process occurs out of our awareness, it consumes enormous amounts of energy. In fact, *fatigue* is a common symptom of emotional suppression. Look for these common dream symbols suggesting that you may be investing excessive energy in hiding your true feelings:

+ Lack of or difficulty with intimacy
+ Separation of any kind

- Weaknesses or unsolvable problems
- Embarrassment
- Feeling self-conscious and insecure
- Confusion, lack of clarity, fuzzy dreams
- Hiding or concealing a mistake

Self-Consciousness

Dreams of vulnerability emerge when we're feeling overly *self-conscious* or *insecure*. These dream feelings are *real* and appear when we deny or suppress these painful waking emotions.

Dreams of insecurity tend to recur over a lifetime. Self-confidence, a belief in ourselves, is nurtured from infancy through adolescence and carried into adulthood. Insecure children tend to grow into insecure adults.

These dreams are usually of mild to moderate emotional intensity but occur regularly, as frequently as every night.

Because of their frequency, we can become desensitized to them, finding them easy to ignore. And if we also ignore waking feelings of insecurity, we create a state of denial, losing touch with who we are and what we truly feel.

Track your dreams, paying attention to your dream emotions over time. If you sense a *pervasive* theme of insecurity, feeling much less confident on the inside than what you portray on the outside, look forward to a discovery process, exploring who you *really* are. If your dreams only occasionally feel insecure, then it's likely that recent events may be temporarily draining your sense of personal confidence. Either way, remember that believing in oneself creates a positive reality of self-understanding.

CHAPTER TWO

Dreaming for Health and Healing

﹏ We can no longer ignore the diagnostic and healing power of dreams. These are *somatic dreams,* meaning they are about the body, and they represent a welcome breadth of knowledge of the power of dreams. It's not surprising that dreams reflect our bodily conditions, our states of health and illness, but it is surprising that these dreams have been overlooked for so long.

Thousands of cases have been documented by dream investigators all over the world, demonstrating the diagnostic, healing, and therapeutic nature of dreams. Several researchers have cataloged dreams typical of various medical conditions and illnesses. Others have focused on the diagnostic and preventative value of dreams, how they help keep us healthy and warn of coming illness. Still others investigate how dreams predict recuperation, suggest treatment, and perhaps most important, actually help heal a wounded body.

My dreams create a reality of health and healing when I accept the power of dreams to change my body.

What Are the
Symbols of the Body?

Most dream systems include metaphors for the human body even if they don't directly address issues of health and healing. Buildings, often the physical features of a *house*, symbolize various body parts:

- Front door: frontal body orifices, such as mouth or vagina
- Back door: posterior body orifice, the anus
- Windows: eyes
- Staircase: spine
- Kitchen: stomach
- Electrical wiring: nervous system
- Chimney: penis

The physical condition of the dream structure is usually believed to represent the condition of the symbolized body part. A broken staircase, for example, may suggest injury to the spine. Clouded or dirty windows may mean your eyesight is strained or compromised. An unusually tall chimney suggests an erection; an unusually short one, concerns about penis size.

These dreams teach us to notice whatever might be unusual or stand out in an image. Was the dream house orderly or was it unkempt? Were there objects lying about? Was the house attractive? Large? Small? Was it well cared for?

The danger with these interpretations is that they rely too heavily on visual images, such as chimney size and proportion, and lose the *feelings* associated with the symbolism. Remember, dream reality is about what you *feel* in a dream, *not* what you see.

Bodily Functions

Some dream systems take a more functional approach, focusing on the actives typical of various regions of a house in order to symbolize body function:

- Bedroom: sleep, sex
- Living room: relaxation
- Kitchen: digestion
- Bathroom: emotional release
- Windows: understanding, insight
- Attic: thought—neurological

These metaphors seem to make more sense for most dreamers but still rely on the visual quality of a dream and therefore can sometimes be misleading.

Freud's famous cigar, probably the ultimate phallic symbol, laid the foundation for nearly unlimited bodily metaphors. Cups are vaginas, seeds are teeth or sperm, wine is blood, mountains represent breasts—the list of this popular symbolism is almost endless.

Likewise there are an unlimited variety of intuitively appealing psychodynamic interpretations for nearly every body part and ailment. For example, constipation symbolizes holding emotion, pulmonary disorders are getting something off the chest, rotting teeth relate to aging or suffering. As appealing as some of these interpretations may seem, if you don't *feel* their reality, they're not real. Symbols of health and healing can take any visual form.

My dreams create a reality of health and healing when I feel my body in my dreams in any form of symbolism.

Sometimes anatomical dream images directly symbolize their physical counterparts. A dream hand represents a physical hand, dreaming of your heart symbolizes your cardiovascular system, dreams of head pain reflect a headache.

One dreamer with gnarled hands from years of osteoarthritis continually dreamed that his hands were being squeezed and deformed by a vise. Another found that dreaming of a creature surrounding and attacking her head signaled the onset of a migraine headache.

So if a dream suggests discomfort or suffering, it would seem wise to at least consider that the afflicted body part requires attention.

It doesn't matter which dream system you find most appealing or which symbols you believe best represent the body since it's not the images alone that create dream reality. Any imagery that you sense is somatic—that is, of the body—be it a house, a cup, or a body part itself, is important. Always attend to the feelings and impressions of your dream—a somatic dream is *any* dream where you feel your body is being symbolized.

Somatic Dreams Have a Distinctive Feel

Most who have experienced somatic dreams related to illness or injury find them unmistakable. Dreams feel different when we're sick. Hospitalized patients, when asked about their dreams, often report dream experiences with a heavier, more somber tone—one patient described his dreams as *thick*. Some of these changes in dreaming may be due to medication, fever, altered sleep patterns, or other disease-related physiological effects, but whatever the cause, dream reality, like waking reality, changes when we're ill.

Notice your dreams when you are sick, even with just a cold or flu, and compare them with those you have while healthy. Once you begin to experience your dreams on a regular basis, you'll find that the difference is striking.

How Can I Diagnose Illness Through My Dreams?

Dreams that diagnose illness, sometimes called *prodromal* dreams, warn of impending health problems before a disease has been medically identified. They are striking and somewhat rare, but it makes considerable sense to pay attention to them. Ned's dream is an example:

> I dreamed my right hip socket was being inflated with air, as if there were a balloon inside. It was getting bigger and bigger until I saw my hip being pushed out of place. . . .

Ned's dream occurred for months prior to his experiencing any physical symptoms. Although his dream was of little concern, he found it odd because it seemed unusually vivid and distinctive, and he even recalls feeling slight pain in his leg on the nights that this dream occurred.

However, a few months later he began to experience moderate pain in his right leg, the same leg as his dream. This pain progressed until he developed a noticeable limp, which finally prompted him to consult a doctor. CT scans revealed what his dream had diagnosed months earlier—there was a calcified mass growing in his right hip, disrupting it from its socket. The leg pain he felt was referred from his hip.

Ned's experience is not unique. Dr. Bernie Siegel, a surgeon and brilliant healer who has written several excellent books on health, describes a patient with breast cancer who awoke from a dream with the terrifying knowledge that her disease had metastasized to her brain. She dreamed that her head was shaved and the word *cancer* was written on it. A few weeks later the diagnosis was confirmed.

Another author reported the case of a man who dreamed that he had been shot in the chest—he saw his heart pierced with blood flowing out of his body and had the sense that a bomb was exploding within him. The medical diagnosis was an arterial infarct, a blocked artery to the heart, during the night.

There are many other striking examples:

- A dreamer turned into a stone statue forewarned a catatonic state
- Dreams of being shot in the head predicted a migraine
- Odd, immobilized wax figures foretold a coma induced by thyroid disease
- Dreaming of floating in dirty water predicted dysentery
- Wiggling, incandescent worms diagnosed the onset of retinal disease months before doctors detected the problem

However, while startling anecdotal stories abound in scientific papers, dream books, popular magazine articles, and television specials, these high-profile, unmistakable prodromal dreams are actually rare. We're given the impression that these are the norm, and they make good press, but most people's dreams are not so dramatic.

The Most Common Somatic Dreams
Warn of Excessive Stress

Because dreams are usually understated—that is, they whisper more often than shout—somatic and perhaps even prodromal dreams are more common than we realize. However, we need to listen carefully for them. And it makes sense that we should; after all, if dreams are acutely aware of our psychological state, why shouldn't they also alert us that something is amiss with our body?

So don't be discouraged if your dreams appear less dramatic—most will, but you can still learn to read the state of your body from dreaming. You'll find that the vast majority of your prodromal dreams quietly tell you to slow down, change your lifestyle, or alleviate stress when you've become too busy to pay direct attention to your health.

These common dreams are provoked by the ordinary stress we face each day. But simple daily stressors are deceptive. Losing the car keys, being late for an appointment, and discovering that the sink is clogged all have a detrimental cumulative effect that batters the immune system, sometimes weakening us to the point where illness can take hold.

When stress becomes excessive and your health is threatened, dreaming will warn you. *If you follow your dream's advice, you can often avoid illness by allowing your immune system to do its job and fight off the threatening pathogens.* Ironically, responding to our dreams by making healthful changes never really allows us to confirm the dream's reality, as the illness is avoided.

My dreams create a reality of health and healing when I listen carefully to their quiet healing messages.

Recognizing Prodromal Dreams

Diagnostic dreams sometimes feel prophetic, or what's called *precognitive,* because they appear to tell us something that we haven't discovered using more conventional methods. However, these dreams are not premonitions, as they merely reflect the *current* state of our bodies—most disease processes, exposed by dreaming or otherwise, are usually in full swing long before doctors detect them. It's analogous to dreams that accurately expose our emotional state, such as feeling angry before we recognize how mad we truly are—the anger exists within us, we just haven't consciously discovered it yet.

Recognizing these diagnostic dreams takes some practice, and as always, concentrate on *feeling* your dream's reality. Here is some symbolism typical of diagnostic dreaming:

+ Dreams that feel distinctly different from what is typical for you
+ Recurring dream feeling and images
+ Symbols of health accompanied by symbols of communication, such as a telephone or wires
+ Feeling forewarned by a dream
+ Dream activity that appears odd or different from the usual—perhaps rigid, motionless images or agitated, overactive ones
+ Any dream characters, human or otherwise, that are physically ill or deformed
+ Symbols associated with health risks such as cigarettes or alcohol
+ Symbols of excessive heat, cold, wetness, dryness, or pain

In addition to general symbols that represent overall changes in health, here are some typical indicators of specific disorders:

Cardiovascular disorders:
+ Squeezing or vise on chest
+ Heavy weight on chest
+ References to blood
+ Pain in the chest
+ A wounded heart image

Migraine:
+ Head wounds
+ Unpleasant, jarring, or pounding sensations
+ Flickering or flashing lights
+ Dizziness

Gastrointestinal disorders:
- Stomach wounds
- Dirty water, feces
- Spoiled, sickening food
- Sickly smell

Obstetrics-gynecological:
- Abnormally cold baby
- Threats to an infant
- Malnourished infant
- Symbols of stillbirth or miscarriage

Dreams that fit any of these qualities may be somatic or even prodromal in nature. Obviously dream information should never replace competent medical advice, but if you are experiencing unusual dreams that you feel relate to your health, it would seem wise to discuss them with your doctor.

My dreams create a reality of health and healing when I use them wisely, in conjunction with the advice and treatment of my doctor.

Can My Dreams Predict the Outcome of an Illness?

Prognosis is a medical term meaning likely outcome or predicting of the course of a disease. *Dreaming for health and healing often includes symbols that foretell improving or declining health after a medical diagnosis has been made.* We know from research conducted at medical colleges that dreams can accurately foretell complications and length of recovery from surgery and infectious diseases. I said earlier that the dreams we experience while sick have a distinctive feel; well, buried within these dreams are signs of improvement or decline.

Above all, dreams forecast improving health by returning to what is typical for each dreamer. When your body is recovering, dreams begin to feel less sick, somber, or dark and more like how they usually feel when you're healthy. Dream symbols associated with healing include the following:

- Lush landscapes, birth, new vegetation or animal life
- A dreamer who is physically threatened but is protected or able to escape this threat
- Movement of previously stiff, immobilized images
- New clothing or structures
- Dreams where someone is healing
- A fresh scene or smell in your dreams, such as a crisp, clear morning or fresh sparkling water

Just as dreams can forecast improving health, they may also reflect changes in our body when an illness is escalating. Your dreams may begin to feel darker, more sick. These are commonly reported symbols of deteriorating health:

- Living creatures that appear sick or malnourished
- Structures or dream characters that are in poor condition and deteriorating
- A dreamer who is physically threatened and unable to escape this threat
- A sickly smell in a dream
- Increased frequency of symbols associated with health risks such as cigarettes or alcohol
- Symbols of death, such as cemeteries or funerals, particularly for men
- Symbols of separation or loss, particularly for women

Of course, such symbolism in and of itself is not sufficient to indicate a deteriorating condition, and as always, the *feel* of a dream is most important. Remember that dreams may be prognostic of emotional well-being as much as of physical health—so the first question you should ask yourself is whether you sense you are dreaming for health and healing or for self-understanding.

Can My Dreams Prescribe Remedies for an Illness?

Not only do dreams diagnose and predict progress through the course of an illness, they also prescribe remedies, heal our body, and signal recovery. These dreams inform us of what our body needs and direct us to take the proper action. If this surprises you, then you're underestimating yourself, as in many instances the body knows exactly what it lacks and what is necessary to overcome the infirmity and recuperate.

Actually this process occurs every day in waking consciousness but is so automatic it's taken for granted. Our body tells us when we're hungry or thirsty and, to some extent, *what* we are hungry or thirsty for—roughage, something sweet, or something salty. It also tells us when to sleep, exercise, meditate. Dreaming for health and healing means listening to your body and accepting that it knows what's needed to remedy the illness and return to a state of health.

I said earlier that dreams usually whisper, and while this is true, they do occasionally shout. Dreams of health and healing sometimes shock us in order to get our attention.

In his book, *Our Dreaming Mind*, emminent dream researcher Dr. Robert Van de Castle reports the case of a well-known sleep scientist who pioneered much of the early REM research and how a particularly frightening dream changed his life. This scientist was a heavy cigarette smoker for many years, and though as a physician he knew of the health risks associated with smoking, he avoided thinking about the possible consequences of his addiction. This is his extremely vivid dream:

> I saw an X ray of my lungs and they were full of cancer. My doctor told me that the disease was widespread with metastases throughout the entire lymph system. He said that if I continued to smoke, I would die, and I knew that would mean losing what I cherished most in life—the opportunity to see my children grow up. . . .

When the dreamer awoke, he felt a sense of great joy and relief and believed that he'd been given a second chance to live. He never smoked another cigarette.

Listen to what your body is asking for in your dreams. Accept its wisdom and that it can guide itself on a path of healing. Don't expect your dreams to shout, but instead pay close attention to the subtleties, the quiet messages. Allow yourself to become aware of your personal dream reality so that you can discern the meaning of these important somatic dreams.

My dreams create a reality of health and healing by teaching me to listen to the needs of my body.

Dreams That Heal

We can use the healing power of dreams to assist our body when we are sick. We know that the immune system is highly responsive to the conscious and unconscious mind; we can, for instance, enhance or diminish immune function solely though *conditioning*. We also know that many states of consciousness promote healing—meditation, autogenics, progressive muscle relaxation, biofeedback, hypnosis—all have proven immune-enhancing properties.

However, dreaming may be a more effective healing state of consciousness because it is the most pure, having full, unblocked access to the unconscious mind. And the unconscious is connected to every bit of us—every invading pathogen, every immune cell that courses our body. Our dreams know our health far better than we can be consciously aware or our doctors can detect even with sensitive instruments.

To believe that dreams *only read* our internal psychological, physical, and spiritual states seems naive. As science and philosophy have shown, it is impossible to observe without altering. Merely becoming aware of our feelings and behavior changes them. Since dreams connect us to the unconscious, we are able to create a reality of health and healing through desire, strengthening and promoting immune response.

Empowering dreams with therapeutic potency is also not a new idea. It dates to ancient times and appears in virtually all cultures where dreamwork is taken seriously. In societies without the benefit of modern medical technology, dream healing and other rituals often exclusively constitute medical treatment.

The Healing Power of Dream Incubation

The most powerful way to create a reality of healing is through *dream incubation.* Incubating a dream means providing self-suggestions for a dream's content and power. It is a form of self-hypnosis, a conditioning process where we cultivate receptiveness to positive, life-affirming suggestions.

Incubation is based on an ancient ritual where a dreamer poses a question before sleep in hopes that a deity will answer in a dream. In ancient Egypt, where incubation was widely practiced, dreams were often incubated in temples erected for *Serapis,* the god of dreaming. An individual may spend weeks traveling to a temple for a single night's sleep in order to obtain guidance. Or, if he was unable to make the trip, a *surrogate dreamer* was sent in his place.

Modern incubation techniques are similar in practice, but without superstition. They are used most frequently to create a personal reality of self-understanding by cutting through emotional defenses and barriers and revealing feelings and beliefs that have eluded conscious awareness. But incubation can also be used to inform us of the condition of our body, strengthen our immune response, promote healing, and obtain comfort and pain relief.

You can create a reality of health and healing through dream incubation by first asking yourself what it is that you are seeking:

- Do you wish to know the state of your health?
- Do you wish guidance as to what your body needs?
- Are you seeking comfort or relief?
- Do you wish to program your dreams with healing powers?

Prepare by choosing one affirmation for a night's sleep that directly addresses your concern. Questions, requests, and affirmations are best kept short, unambiguous, and positive. Crystallize the affirmation clearly in your mind and repeat it quietly to yourself over and over as you are falling asleep. Here are some possible affirmations:

Healing questions:
What shall I do to enhance my healing?
How can I get well?

Am I ready to resume my regular activities?
What is the condition of my body?
How do I strengthen my body and my immune system?

Healing requests:
Please bring me comfort.
Please bring me peace and tranquillity.
Please bring me relief from pain.
Please bring me hope.

Healing affirmations:
I am building a strong and invincible immune system.
My strength is growing through the power of my dreams.
My strength and healing powers are unlimited.
My dreams affirm my body's healthful state.

My dreams create a reality of health and healing when I allow my affirmations to strengthen my body and bring me comfort.

Incubation can be done *visually* as well as verbally. For many, visualizations feel more natural, seem easier, and therefore better condition the unconscious mind than verbal affirmations. The choice depends solely on what feels best for you.

The visual incubation process is identical to what I have just described except that visual images replace affirmations. While falling asleep, picture the image as clearly as possible in your mind and allow yourself to submerge within this visualization. Don't be a passive observer, as if you were *watching* a movie; instead become a part of the scene, see it flowing over you, around you, within you.

There are an unlimited number of healing visualizations that you can use. Some are general and have no specific connection to any illness while others include the affected body part within the image. Symbols of *water* seem to have particular healing (as well as spiritual) benefits, so if they feel right to you, include them.

Here are some visualizations based on suggestions by Dr. Patricia Garfield, author of *The Healing Power of Dreams* and one of the world's leading dream experts, as well as other dreamworkers:

GENERAL HEALING VISUALIZATIONS:
A gentle breeze bringing fresh, clean air . . .
Free-floating in a pool of sparkling clear water . . .
A soothing massage . . .
Feelings of love filling every part of your body . . .
A peaceful stroll on a beautiful clear beach . . .
Flying peacefully over clear waters . . .
Feelings of peace flowing through your body . . .

VISUALIZATIONS FOR CARDIOVASCULAR DISORDERS:
A swing swaying easily in a calm, rhythmic fashion . . .
Soft music that washes rhythmically over the body . . .

VISUALIZATIONS FOR GASTROINTESTINAL DISORDERS:
A soothing potion that calms the stomach . . .
Cool, clear water rinsing the abdomen . . .
Wrapping the stomach in a soft, clean, comfortable cloth . . .

VISUALIZATIONS FOR ARTHRITIC DISORDERS:
Skating freely and gracefully across ice, water, or air . . .
Dancing or walking with fluid, gliding movements . . .

VISUALIZATIONS FOR PULMONARY DISORDERS:
Breathing easily while inhaling steam from a kettle . . .
Deep breaths of crisp, pure mountain air . . .

VISUALIZATIONS FOR OBSTETRICS AND GYNECOLOGICAL DISORDERS:
Warming and nurturing an infant . . .
Cherishing an infant, rocking, soothing, comforting the baby . . .
New birth flooded with radiant light and sparkling water . . .
Making passionate, satisfying love . . .

VISUALIZATIONS FOR MIGRAINE:
Warming hands with a cup of steaming hot tea . . .
Relaxing on a cool dim evening . . .
A cool gentle breeze caressing your head . . .

VISUALIZATIONS FOR PAIN:
Pain melting like butter, dripping slowly out of your body . . .
Pain changing colors, becoming lighter and fading . . .
Pain evaporating, like steam, out of the affected body part . . .

> My dreams create a reality of health and healing when I allow
> my visualizations to boost my immune system and relieve my
> pain.

Naturally, the healing power of affirmations and visualizations should never be used to *replace* traditional medical care. Those who advocate a return to the past are as shortsighted as those who believe that the past has nothing to teach us. Using your dreams to create a reality of health and healing is a powerful *adjunct* to modern medicine.

The Powerful Effect of Emotions on Our Health

We create a reality of health and healing when we acknowledge the powerful way that *emotions* affect our body. Internalizing unpleasant feelings such as anger, frustration, or resentment tears down our immune system, making us vulnerable to disease. Research has shown that we can predict cardiovascular disease, cancer, neurological disorders, and many other diseases by our tendency to suppress unpleasant feelings. Likewise, allowing ourselves to experience moments of joy and happiness promotes healing and physical well-being. Laughter, for instance, is a potent antidote to illness.

Dreams are our clearest, most direct connection to our emotional selves, giving us honest feedback on the state of our feelings. We can use this valuable information to identify feelings that haven't been released and that fester and eventually compromise our health.

> My dreams create a reality of health and healing when I
> recognize that my emotions powerfully affect my health.

I said above that as we recover from sickness our dreams return to the style and tone of what they were prior to our illness. They begin to loose that distinctive sickly feel and gradually regain normalcy. Dreams of recovery may also include symbols of sparkling water, or new life, clothing, or structures. If our infirmed body part appears in a dream, it may look more healthy and intact.

Our dreams may still contain symbols of medical treatments as well as other images associated with our illness, particularly if these procedures were painful or frightening. But these unpleasant dreams will soon decrease in frequency, weaken in potency, and become less threatening. Occasionally nightmares may persist, usually if the disease had its traumatic moments, but these nightmares are more related to the psychological trauma caused by the disease than to physical health and healing. In this case the body is recovering faster than the mind.

Dreams of Chronic Illness

Illnesses that are particularly severe or long-standing can change the character of our dreams in such a way that we almost forget what our dreams felt like prior to the sickness. But when our normal, premorbid dreams return, they feel pleasant, familiar, and welcome. They are signs that we are returning to a state of health.

Many of the prognostic symbols indicating improvement that I mentioned earlier may be prominent as the body begins to win its battle against illness. You may also notice that as your health improves, your dreams will once again reflect everyday needs and desires not associated with your illness, such as sexual dreams or the return of a common theme that had been pushed aside as the disease commanded your attention.

These are all positive signs that signal recovery and return to your preillness state. Dreaming for health and healing means being sensitive to these signs, taking heart in them, which in turn further strengthens your body's natural immune defenses.

My dreams create a reality of health and healing when I am sensitive to the wondrous signs that my body is healing and my immune defenses are strengthening.

The Six Symbols of Health and Healing

- ◆ Anger
- ◆ Balance
- ◆ Body
- ◆ Joy
- ◆ Risk
- ◆ Stress

Symbols of Anger

Anger is as much about health as it is self-understanding because of the powerful effect it has on our body. Medical research suggests that *internalized or unexpressed anger* is one of the best predictors of heart attacks, perhaps even better than diet or genetic factors. Anger also changes and deteriorates the lining of the stomach by promoting secretion of acids as well as increasing the likelihood and severity of other stress-related diseases. Perhaps most important, those who carry their anger within are far more likely to die sooner than those who do not.

Stuffing anger, burying it deep enough so that we and others are unaware of its presence, never rids us of it. It exists below the level of consciousness, churning and, over time, tearing us up inside. Dreams of anger are often a warning that we've internalized this powerful emotion.

On the other hand, externalized anger, openly and indiscriminately expressed, has greater psychological and social effects than health consequences, but the costs are still enormous: distancing relationships, regret, alienation leading to loneliness, guilt, bitterness.

My dreams create a reality of health and healing by acknowledging the powerful effect that anger has on my body.

Angry feelings were meant to be experienced and released, not hidden or repressed. And as with all emotions, anger is not necessarily bad but is sometimes useful. *Anger warns us that something is wrong.* It protects us, mobilizing us to escape or defend ourselves in times of physical danger. It tells us when boundaries are violated, when we are being pushed beyond what is appropriate, when we need to set limits, or when we are being taken advantage of. It helps us overcome fear, as it's easier to assert our needs when we feel angry. Anger also protects us from other feelings that at the moment may be psychologically overwhelming—helplessness, loneliness, sadness.

But to be psychologically effective and physically benign, we need to experience our anger and move on. This does not necessarily mean *venting.* Contrary to popular belief, venting anger is not always healthy, particularly at someone else's expense. Once angry feelings are openly expressed, they can scar and are impossible to take back. While venting is not always healthy, *experiencing* angry feelings is— and stuffing them is physically harmful.

My dreams create a reality of health and healing when I relinquish the need to hold my anger.

Finding anger in a dream is usually as simple as *feeling* it. But symbols of anger can take more latent forms:

- Dream feelings that range from irritation to rage
- A recurring theme of being confronted by enemies
- A wish to punish your dream enemy
- Recurring themes of injustice, blame, or selfishness
- Recurring, overly aggressive dream feelings
- Unusually loud dreams
- Feeling in a dream as if you're burning up inside

Symbols of the body, particularly the *abdomen,* occasionally represent anger. A distended abdomen reflects internalized anger, feelings held inside instead of being expressed that are affecting your health.

An exposed abdomen accompanied by brittle or weak feelings symbolizes physical vulnerability. Just as an animal protects its defenseless underbelly when it senses danger, your subconscious may be warning you not to overexpose yourself—you may be stretching yourself too thin, jeopardizing your health.

My dreams create a reality of health and healing when I accept my dream anger as a signal to experience and release feelings of anger and hostility.

Symbols of Balance

Dreams of balance are the most difficult health and healing dreams to describe because they represent an unfamiliar and misunderstood concept. Balance means *moderation,* taking all things, but taking them in reasonable doses. It is our body's natural state of equilibrium compensating for physical and emotional excess.

Balance is fundamental to creating a reality of health and healing, and life stress often disrupts our physical balance. We overeat, over-drink, work too much, sit too much, hurry too much, stew in anger too much. We're pressed with deadlines so that little else matters. And we engage in this lifestyle without compensating by relaxation, quiet time, healthy food, exercise, and spiritual pursuits. When we become physically imbalanced, we increase our susceptibility to ill-ness.

My dreams create a reality of health and healing by restoring my natural state of balance.

Dreaming for health and healing restores the natural balance that is disrupted during waking reality. Dreams are self-regulating; they compensate for physical and psychological excess, promote uncon-scious healing, and inform us when our emotional reactions are dis-proportionate to their cause.

Dreams warning of imbalance usually have an unsettling feeling, as if something is wrong, unfair, or not symmetrical. For instance:

- Excessive fear
- Dream objects that are out of proportion, overly large or small
- Distances that seem to stretch
- Lopsided images: for example, a scale out of balance
- Obviously unfair play
- Music out of harmony

Dreams of balance are both a warning and a form of compensation for excessive waking emotions or behavior. It's been said that dreams are an unappreciated natural resource because they help restore the balance that is disrupted during waking reality. To increase awareness of what you can do to restore your body's harmony, at bedtime program your dreams with an affirmation such as the following:

I seek balance in my life.
What changes can I make to bring the scales more in balance?
I am in a state of harmony and balance.

Symbols of the Body

Dreaming for health and healing means learning to recognize how your body is symbolized in a dream. As I discussed above, the body may take any form of dream symbolism, but it is most commonly represented either *anatomically* or by the *metaphor of a structure*. However, if you *feel* your body is being symbolized regardless of the visual form, it likely is.

In many somatic dreams anatomical images and their related function have health and healing symbolism:

Abdomen	Emotion
Arms	Fine motor skills, coordination
Back, spine	Physical strength, stamina
Brain	Neurological disorders
Breast	Female sexuality, obstetric concerns
Buttocks	Bowel function

Chest	Cardiovascular system
Ear	Hearing
Eye	Vision
Face	Dermatological concerns—acne, self-perception, concerns of how illness changes appearance
Foot	Movement
Hair	Protection, self-perception, concerns of how illness changes appearance
Hand	Fine motor skills, coordination
Head	Neurological concerns
Heart	Cardiovascular system
Leg	Strength, movement
Lungs	Pulmonary disease
Mouth	Gastrointestinal system, digestion
Nose	Smell
Penis	Male sexuality
Shoulders	Strength, stamina
Skin	Immunity, protection from invading pathogens
Teeth	Dental concerns, digestion
Vagina	Gynecological concerns

Seeing a human body in a dream doesn't by itself make a dream somatic. The body may represent anything depending on the feel of the dream and, in fact, often is a *psychological* symbol. Dream bodies may refer to emotional strength and our social support system, such as friends, family, or church. A strong, intact image signifies a solid social support structure; a weak body represents a yearning for closer and stronger ties to those around you.

Dreams of the body may take the form of a building or structure as well. Symbols of the entire edifice represent the body in total, but still consider the *function* of the structure to interpret its health and healing meaning. For instance:

Restaurant	Gastrointestinal function
Office	Neurological concerns
Hotel	Rest or sexuality
Hospital	Acute health concerns
Prison	Chronic illness, trapped, helpless

More commonly, dreams of health and healing are symbolized by a single room or part of a building, with the structure's physical features analogous to various bodily functions. For example:

Bedroom	Sleep, sex
Living room	Relaxation
Kitchen	Digestion
Bathroom	Gastrointestinal function
Windows	Vision
Attic	Neurological concerns

However, always attend to the feelings and impressions of your dream—a somatic dream is *any* one that you sense your body is being symbolized.

Once you have identified a dream as somatic, listen to what it is telling you about your body:

- Is this a diagnostic dream, warning of an incubating illness?
- Is your dream cautioning you to make lifestyle changes?
- Is this a prognostic dream, informing you of improvement or decline?
- Is this dream a part of your body's natural healing process?

Look for the subtle messages in somatic dreams. For instance, recurring symbols that are initially frail, but seem to gain strength with each repeated dream, are signs of healing. Also, consider how this dream fits with other symbols as well as your waking behavior in order to create a personal reality of health and healing.

Symbols of Joy

Joy is our most powerful healing emotion. Pioneering work in the new medical discipline of *psychoneuroimmunology* has documented how this simple emotion successfully combats diseases as common as the flu and as virulent as cancer.

Dreams of joy may take different forms; to recognize them, look for these recurring symbols:

- Dreams that feel fun, or where dream characters are having fun
- Joyous laughter in a dream
- Dreams that feel unhurried, unpressured, or at ease
- Dreams that have a feel of contented simplicity
- Themes of unselfishness, giving, or appreciation

Ask yourself how these dreams of joy fit with your *waking* reality. Have you been having as much fun as you'd like lately? Have you been able to really laugh? Have you had opportunity to experience moments of feeling unpressured, unhurried? Have you had the time to appreciate simplicity? Have you been smiling? All of these promote health, and your dream may be a gentle nudge in this direction.

Dreams of Joy Are Signs of Healing

While you are recovering from illness, dreams of joy are both a sign of improvement and a strengthening of the body. Look at the context of your dream over several nights: Are your dreams losing a distinctive sick feeling? Before they return to what is typical for you, dreams of joy may be buried signs that your body is healing. Also look for additional prognostic symbolism: new life, lush landscapes, fresh sparkling water, or a physically safe and protected feeling or dreams where images of healing occur.

Dreaming for joy is healing because it increases susceptibility to waking feelings of contented happiness. Laughter, humor, kindness, appreciation, and a sense of connectedness are powerful antidotes to disease.

Sadly, cultivating a joyous attitude in waking life has become a lost art. Fortunately, however, a joyful dream reality compensates for these waking deficiencies. The changes are subtle, but as you create your dreams of joy, you'll find yourself conjuring more pleasant memories, doing more just for fun, and spending more moments finding the simple beauty that surrounds you.

No one can force these feelings, but you can allow them to unfold.

Program your dreams for joy using affirmations that increase your susceptibility to joyousness:

I allow myself to enjoy each moment.
I allow myself to be spontaneous, joyous, and cheerful.
I allow myself frequent, overwhelming episodes of appreciation.
I allow myself to connect with others and nature.
I allow my heart to smile.

Choose whichever affirmation feels best for you and relax, repeating it quietly to yourself at bedtime.

Dreams of joy compensate for stress and illness by creating joyful images and feelings. Dream compensation such as this reflects *unconscious healing,* as the inner self gradually restores balance, repairing the body and mind. Think of the unconscious mind as fluid, like a body of water. If disrupted, it works to regain homeostasis, its most natural and comfortable state, where physical and psychological extremes such as illness, stress, sadness, or anger are countered by healthfulness, joy, and forgiveness.

My dreams create a reality of health and healing when I seek to fill my life with joy.

Symbols of Risk

Risk means increasing our vulnerability to illness or injury by an excessive, destructive, or careless lifestyle. Dreams of risk warn us about the consequences of our behavior in a way that no other state of consciousness can.

The most common dreams of risk are those that include symbols of unhealthy or high-risk waking behaviors:

+ Alcohol or drugs
+ Smoking or other tobacco use
+ High-risk sexual behavior

- Reckless or high-risk recreational behavior
- Overeating

This symbolism indicates that the manner in which you are coping may be holding psychological tension at bay but is taking a toll on your body.

Excessive alcohol use, for example, goes beyond what is socially or recreationally acceptable and becomes a way of denying inner anxiety. Unfortunately the effects are emotionally temporary and, over time, physically harmful. It may seem more painful to confront fears directly, as anxiety thrives on avoidance, but if faced squarely, they will diminish and your body will respond positively in kind.

Dreams of risk may also indicate a need to take greater responsibility for your behavior. Something you are doing has health consequences that you should be aware of. Ask yourself if you've been under excessive stress lately. Are you overeating? Is your sleep adequate? Are you getting sufficient exercise? Are you engaging in high-risk behaviors? Your dream suggests a need for lifestyle change, relaxation, quiet time, and greater simplicity in your life. Once you start the small steps of change, listen to your dreams for symbols of strength and improvement.

My dreams create a reality of health and healing when I listen for my vulnerabilities and allow myself healthful changes.

Symbols of Stress

Creating a reality of health and healing means listening to dream advice even when it is softly spoken. If we listen carefully, dreams will tell us about our body's needs well before we notice these needs consciously. This is a great opportunity, as it allows us to avoid the physical harm that can accompany chronic psychological and physical stress.

Dreams of stress alert us to the accumulation of daily tension, the crippling health consequences of which are well-known, and should be considered an early warning to change your lifestyle.

Stress may come from *anywhere* or, more likely, from *everywhere*. If you watch yourself closely, you will see the signs that your dream is revealing:

♦ *You may be surprised to realize just how hurried you are.*
For most of us, hurrying has become a habit, but such a common one that it feels natural, a normal part of our lives. We are also surrounded by others who hurry, we expect others to hurry, and slowing down becomes a major conscious effort.

♦ *You may recognize how you have neglected your body.*
It's all too easy to take our health for granted. We often neglect our body until it troubles us, and physical deterioration is usually a gradual, barely noticeable process. It's also easy to fall into the seductive trap of overeating, overdrinking, and underexercising—most of us do. Convenience replaces health, and putting off healthful resolutions until tomorrow often means that changes never seem to happen.

♦ *You may be more worried than you realize.*
Worrying is also a habit. Like hurrying, it becomes chronic, feels natural, and seems commonplace. We worry about finances that are barely manageable, expectations that are unmeetable, demands that are unreasonable—this is the stuff of everyday life, so common we expect it, yet it takes a toll on our body.

Dreams of stress alert us to the importance of protecting our health; as our stress builds, so does our need for relaxation, joy, and simplicity.

My dreams create a reality of health and healing when I recognize the stress in my life and allow myself the opportunity for relaxation, joy, and simplicity.

CHAPTER THREE

Dreaming for Relationships

It is written in the Book of Genesis that in the beginning God created the heavens and the earth and then created man in His own likeness. But knowing that it was not good for man to be alone, God placed Adam in a deep sleep, took a rib from his side, and fashioned woman, so that man and woman could join and become one flesh.

This biblical parable teaches the importance of relationships. Humans *need* one another. From our very inception, the product of a joining of two people, we are social creatures woven together in a web of personal and professional interaction. For the most part we are dependent upon each other for our physical and emotional survival.

Why Do We Need Companionship?

Our first relationship, that with our parents, provides the physical and emotional needs that we as infants were incapable of supplying for ourselves—food, water, protection, nurturing. As we grow, we seek out friends and then mates to supply us with what we cannot—a complement to our physical and emotional strengths and weaknesses. We share with others our struggles and triumphs, we listen, we hope, we care, we want to be cared about. Even our professional relationships supply more than the material necessities of life—they are a human connection as well as a source of status and identity.

Dreams of relationships are common because relationships are so important to us. Not surprisingly, most of these dreams involve intimate relationships. We can learn from our dreams how we feel about others and what our needs are and obtain guidance in cultivating healthy, lasting relationships.

As with all dreams, dreams of relationships are meaningful when they are *felt*. These feelings will be different for each of us because our need for companionship differs, but use the following as an interpretive guide:

+ *When you love someone:*
    Feel or sense love, caring, or self-sacrifice in a dream, regardless of the dream imagery

+ *When you do not love someone:*
    Dreams that feel distant, uncaring, or nothing at all

+ *Fear of loss or hurt in a relationship:*
    Dreams that feel excessively clingy or needy
    Dream characters emotionally or physically attached, *joined at the hip*

+ *Anger in a relationship:*
    Dreams that feel angry, aggressive, or frustrated
    Feeling vulnerable, unprotected, or helpless in a dream

+ *If you are not getting your needs met:*
    Dreams that feel needy or a sense of longing
    Yearning for human connection or touch

+ *Coping with loss or a relationship that is ending:*
    Dreams that feel grief-stricken

+ *Need for greater independence:*
    Feeling smothered in a dream
    Dream characters emotionally or physically attached, *joined at the hip*

+ *Need for nurturing:*
  Feeling lonely or mildly afraid in a dream
  Feeling needy

What Is the Importance of Communication?

Communication is an interpersonal exchange of thoughts, messages, and feelings. It is both *expression* as well as *listening,* and it is the cornerstone of all relationships; without verbal and nonverbal dialogue we cannot interact with one another. The quality of our communication often determines the quality of our relationships.

There are probably more symbols associated with communication than any other theme in our dreams. Symbols of communication are apparent by their imagery—what we typically think of as *devices of communication* emerge symbolically in dreams. For example:

+ advertisement	+ ink	+ pager
+ antenna	+ language	+ paper
+ book	+ letter	+ pen
+ computer	+ library	+ pencil
+ envelope	+ magazine	+ telegram
+ fax	+ newspaper	+ telephone

Some symbols of communication may be less obvious yet still quite common:

+ codes	+ handshake	+ lock and key
+ deaf or mute	+ kissing	+ mazes
+ eyes	+ listening	+ touch

The *quality* of our waking communication is revealed by our dream feelings. Poor communication is often felt in dreams as frustration, helplessness, worry, or anger.

I was talking on the phone to my mother and there was so much static on the line, I could barely hear what she was saying. I knew she was telling me something important, but I was worried because I couldn't make out what it was. . . .

The dreamer's phone call is a classic dream of communication, while the conversation disrupted by static on the phone line suggests difficulty communicating. The dreamer's quality of communication is also revealed by the dream's feelings—worried and helpless.

Not surprisingly, when communication is strained, symbols of *communication* and *stress* may appear together in dreams. Instead of speaking, there will be yelling or deafness. Conflict such as fighting or sparring but without a sense of power is common. Duels, warfare, wrestling, silence, confrontation, or other symbols of stress frequently emerge in dreams of troubled communication, as will feelings of helplessness, tension, or frustration.

Without a doubt, the number one complaint that marriage counselors face is poor communication. Even in healthy relationships it is easy to become so preoccupied with daily hassles and stress that we miss what our partner is trying to tell us. Listening may be our most important communication skill, and it is certainly the most difficult to master. Fortunately what we don't consciously *hear* is still being processed unconsciously, and dreams can alert us to what we are missing. Be attentive to these dream symbols, as they suggest that an important message has been overlooked:

+ Listening but not doing in a dream
+ Deafness or blindness
+ Blank pages
+ Shouting
+ Emphatic messages, such as huge writing
+ Any dream that feels like something is missing

If you notice these symbols, consider that you may be losing an important waking message. Of course, it is usually best to ask your partner directly, but if you're unable to do this, incubate your dreams for clear advice. At bedtime seed your dreams with affirmations such as these:

I am open to the message being told me.
I am free to hear what is being said.

I seek honest and truthful communication.
I allow my unconscious mind to speak to me.
My dreams are a source of deep meaning and understanding.

What About Love and Intimacy in My Dreams?

Dreams of love and intimacy are usually subtle and frequently lack the actual image of our lovers. Instead their imagery seems to be more symbolic:

+ Bells and other jubilant sounds
+ Calming scenes such as the ocean, beach, or landscapes
+ Cupid's arrow or other symbols you associate with love
+ Festive joining, marriage
+ New life or growth

Dreams of love *feel* loving, happy, content, serene, not melancholic. They are not loud but also not overly subdued; they seem to glow quietly. They are pleasant, the kinds of dreams you don't wish to wake from.

Intimacy

The great psychologist Erik Erikson once described intimacy as *finding oneself yet losing oneself in another.* Sadly, such intimacy seems more and more difficult to achieve. However, we crave it whether we realize it or not and sometimes mistakenly try to satisfy our intimacy needs with sexual interactions. Naturally this never works—sex is not intimacy—so we continue an unconscious, sometimes frantic search to fill this emotional void.

When intimacy needs are not being met, expect to feel this void in your dreams. Here is some telling dream symbolism:

+ *A need for intimacy:*
    Feeling alone, isolated
    Cold, rigid personal interactions
    Yearning for something but unable to obtain it

+ *Compensating for a lack of intimacy in waking reality:*
    Feelings of comfort, closeness, and safety
    Loving, intimate imagery
    Soothing imagery and feelings unrelated to relationships

+ *Dreams of intimacy warn when you fear you are losing intimacy:*
    Partner or dream symbolism that feels very distant
    Imagery that appears far off in the distance

Loving Yourself

Dreams of love remind us to love ourselves. Self-love is essential to healthy relationships and should never be confused with conceit or selfishness. In fact, we could modify the Golden Rule to read *Do unto yourself as you would have others do unto you.*

When we neglect or mistreat ourselves, we are alerted by dreams of love that feel insecure, hurt, lonely, or victimized regardless of imagery. We may also dream of power, a form of compensation, although these dreams will seem hollow and unfulfilling. In addition, be attentive to this symbolism:

+ Slow, unsure movements
+ Embarrassment
+ Distinct feelings of insecurity
+ Putting on a front, feeling as if you're hiding your true self
+ Shrinking or unusually small images

Learn to love yourself by programming your dreams for an abundance of self-love. Incubate dreams by using affirmations such as the following at bedtime:

I allow myself to love myself.
I am free to love who I am.

*I am a special person; there is no one in the universe like me.
God loves me unconditionally.*

My dreams create a reality of relationships when I give myself
permission to love myself unconditionally.

Loving Others

Dreams of love also expose our style of loving toward a partner.
This can be valuable feedback for us, particularly when we enter a
relationship with someone whose style differs from our own. As with
all dreams, imagery is less important than emotion for interpreting
meaning, so it's important to be attentive to the variety of *feelings*
associated with these dreams of love:

+ *Dreams that symbolize romantic love:*
   Feels warm, emotional, cuddling, sexual

+ *Dreams that symbolize friendship love:*
   Feels as if you *like* someone, but not romantic love
   Feels comfortable, safe

+ *Dreams that symbolize needy love:*
   Feels clingy, possessive, insecure, jealous

+ *Dreams that symbolize martyr love:*
   Feels other centered, self-sacrificing yet shallow, like a
      martyr

+ *Dreams that symbolize intellectual love:*
   Feels cool, passionless, sterile

+ *Dreams that symbolize self-centered love:*
   Feels selfish, distant, lacks intimacy

> My dreams create a reality of relationships when I accept that once I love myself I am free to love and be loved by others.

What Do My Sexual Dreams Mean?

Sexual dreams are among the most common of all dreams—virtually everyone has them regardless of age, gender, sexual orientation, or attitudes about sex. Unfortunately, because of our societal taboo against acknowledging sexual imagery and fantasies in dreams, they frequently lead to feelings of guilt or shame.

But it is important to remember that we create sexual dreams; they represent who we are. If we're not comfortable with our dreams, we cannot be comfortable with ourselves.

Sexual dreams are never meant to shock or embarrass. No matter how strange they may seem, there's nothing unhealthy, abnormal, or obscene about these dreams. They guide and teach us—about our own sexuality as well as our relationships. These dreams often reflect the maturity and quality of our sexual lives.

Such was the case with Sandra, the wife of a church leader, conservative, respected, proper, and devoutly religious. She came to me because of a terribly troubling dream, one that she found offensive and extremely embarrassing, and while she had been dreaming it off and on for years, she never dared mention it to anyone.

However, this and similar dreams were beginning to recur with greater frequency over the past few months, to the point where Sandra was starting to worry that there might be something psychologically wrong with her. Bedtime was becoming something of a private ordeal—she feared falling asleep, dreading the dream's reappearance.

As Sandra spoke through her tears, she struggled for euphemisms to avoid sexually loaded words. Here is how she described a fragment of her dream:

> I'm in a cheap hotel room—of course I've never seen it before —it's dark and dirty and has a horrible smell. I'm lying on

this old, rickety bed—with a broken metal bed frame and filthy stained sheets. I'm, well, a prostitute. But the worst part is that I'm doing unspeakable things, you know, sexual things with strange men. . . .

By today's standards Sandra's dream was probably no more explicit than a typical network television movie. But for her it was offensive, repulsive, alien—and inconceivable that she could dream it over and over.

Sandra's dream does reflect dissatisfaction with her sex life, but it doesn't mean that she has a hidden desire to have lurid sex with strange men. As part of her religious beliefs, she felt it her duty—the unspoken duty of a good wife—to please her husband sexually, even at the expense of her own needs and desires. However, a conscious belief, no matter how fervently, even desperately, it's affirmed, will never convince the unconscious to make us feel something that we don't truly feel.

Sandra decided that she needed to talk with her husband about *her* sexual needs. Fortunately it is also church doctrine that husbands honor their wives, and within the context of their loving relationship they were able mutually to improve the quality of their sexual experiences.

Through a dream, Sandra's unconscious mind eventually made its message clear, and because of it she was able to make positive changes in her life. This is the way of dreams—regardless of what we think we *should* feel, dreams will tell us what we *do* feel. They provide a candid, uninhibited view of our most personal feelings and attitudes about ourselves and our sexuality.

My dreams create a reality of relationships when I accept that sexual dreams are normal and natural, to be enjoyed and not feared.

Sexual Dreams Can Be a Barometer of Your Relationships

Sexuality is exquisitely sensitive to changes and conflict in relationships. Think about how vulnerable we are, how easily hurt we can be by a simple disparaging comment about our sexuality, words that in any other context might not offend us.

Dreams of sexuality tell us about our relationships—when they need attention—even before we recognize this in waking reality. Again, dream imagery is less important than a dream's feelings. It doesn't matter *whom* you are having sex with in a dream, so don't feel guilty or embarrassed if it's not your regular partner. In fact, dreams of actually making love to our partners are rare. But, as always, *feel* your dreams; sexual dreams that are suggestive of relationship issues are distinctive:

+ Disgusting or offensive feelings
+ Unpleasant or painful sex
+ Distinctly nonerotic and unarousing, but sex as a duty or chore

Sexual dreams inform us about our sense of sexuality and the quality of our sex lives in the same way that they are a barometer of our relationships. Are our sexual needs being met? Do we feel lacking, hoping for something different or more adventurous? Are we too inhibited to ask for what we really want? When we're uncomfortable with our sexuality, these dream symbols may emerge:

+ Dreams with excessive sexual imagery and feelings
+ Excessively erotic dreams—feels like too much
+ Unarousing sexual dreams
+ Feeling jealous in a sexual dream
+ Disgusting or offensive feelings

Sexual Dreams Can Be a Healthy Emotional Release

Many sexual dreams represent a healthy and desirable emotional and physical release. This is a *catharsis,* a release of tension that renews and restores, allowing us safely to express in dreams what we cannot in waking reality.

Sexuality is our natural state of being. Dreams compensate for the inherent imbalance of denying this part of ourselves in waking reality —in fact, one would expect that a celibate individual's dreams would be richly sexual. The most obvious example of sexual energy being released in dreams is a *nocturnal emission*, or so-called wet dream, which culminates in ejaculation.

If we can learn to accept sexual dreams as a natural and normal part of who we are, if we can lose any guilt that may be associated with them, we can begin to enjoy our sexual dreams, finding in them a great source of pleasure.

How Can My Dreams Help When a Relationship Ends?

Few events in life are more traumatic than ending a relationship. But because this happens so frequently, we tend to overlook the pain of separation. Rejection, divorce, and death of a loved one tear us apart in ways we can never anticipate. Relationships are emotionally binding; we become tightly woven together, not simply attached, so breaking these binds is never neat and clean—it is a jagged, painful process of ripping and tearing.

Loss of a meaningful relationship is always reflected in dreams. Naturally, the more important or long-lasting the relationship, the more difficult the break or loss, the more likely healing will occur in dreams. *Dreams of loss feel grief-stricken.* The imagery can vary, but there is a common theme of loss or painful change:

- Divorce, separation
- Something of value that is lost
- Amputation, surgical removal
- Death or miscarriage
- Ashes

Dreams help us heal the deep emotional wounds of a broken or lost relationship. While we are learning to cope with the great changes that this loss inflicts in waking reality, we are also grieving and healing in our dreams. This process is automatic and unconscious—like the body's ability to repair itself, psychological injuries heal without the need for us to *will* them to do so. There is nothing that we really need to do, but we can watch the process unfold in our dreams. When we are coping, we experience

- dreams of compensation (see the following paragraph).
- grief in our dreams (grief is the emotion of psychological healing).
- problem solving (what we do next to get on with our life).
- comforting imagery, friends, and companionship.

Certain dreams, called *dreams of compensation,* also help heal the pain of loss by restoring emotional balance. The most fundamental of natural laws is that nature seeks balance. From pulsating electrons to the flow of ocean tides to a predator-prey life cycle, all natural things ultimately find rest in equilibrium. Likewise the unconscious mind abhors emotional excess, and dreams help to compensate by restoring emotional balance.

A client of mine, a charming, soft-spoken man in his seventies, sought out psychotherapy to help cope with the recent loss of his wife. Theirs was a cherished, fifty-year relationship that ended abruptly following a brief but catastrophic illness. He tearfully, lovingly described their lives together in a way that would move even the hardest of souls—his wife was his best friend and closest companion, who shared every secret, every part of his life.

My client was understandably sad, lonely, and though he didn't know it, at risk—elderly men who lose a lifelong spouse often die themselves within just a few months. While still in the grips of his depression, he had this dream:

> I was sitting in a most beautiful place—a mountainside covered with tall pine trees and a deep blue alpine lake below. It was a glorious spring day, my favorite time of year. The air was crystal clear, filled with the scent of pines. Billowy white pillow clouds floated against the blue sky. I could feel a slight warm breeze on my face. Squirrels, just like the ones I feed at home, were playing—happily chasing one another and busily gathering twigs. I felt so content, I wanted to stay forever. . . .

My client's dream was a welcome respite from the sweeping emotional shift that rocked his psyche. Through no fault of his own, he had gone too far, swung out of psychological balance—his profound sadness engulfing every small sliver of joy.

Dreams of compensation reflect unconscious healing—the inner self is gradually restoring balance, repairing the psychological damage. Think of the unconscious mind as fluid, like a body of water. If disrupted, it works to regain homeostasis—its most natural and comfortable state. Extremes of sadness are countered by joy, anger is compensated by forgiveness. This is why we sometimes experience dreams of greatly inflated self-image, control, or power. This wonderful psychological drama is acted out every night in our dreams.

My dreams create a reality of relationships by compensating for emotional excesses that threaten my psychological well-being.

Denial and Letting Go

It is often difficult to accept that a cherished relationship has ended. Like it or not, this loss causes great pain, sometimes so much so that we cope with *denial*. Denial is the process of unconsciously creating false hope by ignoring reality, unwittingly refusing to face the truth.

When we are in denial, the reality we accept feels real, but it is not. And when we break free of denial, we can't imagine how we could ever have been so blind.

Unlike waking reality, dreams are never fooled by denial, but they also don't tell us about this defense *directly*. Instead dreams just go about their natural process of repairing the psychological damage that precipitated denial in the first place.

However, repeatedly experiencing dreams of compensation or grief without recognizing any logical connection between these dreams and waking reality is a signal that you are in denial.

My dreams create a reality of relationships when I listen for my true feelings in my dreams.

Disentangling a close relationship is one of the most painful tasks most of us ever experience. Needless to say, when we have difficulty *letting go* it shows up clearly in our dreams. These struggles are commonly symbolized as follows:

- Repetitive dreams with symbolism of former partner
- Anger, bitterness, in dreams
- Emotional or physical binds to a symbol of your former partner
- Sex with former partner
- Clinging to a symbol of your former partner
- Feeling excessively needy or clinging

How Can My Dreams Help Create Healthy Relationships?

Dreams of relationships are powerful in that they help us build healthy and lasting friendships, partnerships, and romantic relationships. They increase awareness of how we feel toward our partner as well as teach us to be better listeners. They keep our relationships emotionally honest by preventing denial, suppression, or jealousy from clouding self-understanding and restraining a growing relationship. Dreaming restores our lost vision, helps us face sometimes painful truths about ourselves, and gives us the persistence to stay and work when our first impulse is to turn and run. Listening to your dreams is an invaluable step in creating a reality of healthy relationships.

We can actively program our dreams for guidance, strength, and growth in relationships by incubating questions and affirmations. Use this powerful process to answer questions that concern you or to facilitate change. Seed your dreams by repeating one of the following affirmations quietly to yourself as you fall asleep over the course of a week:

Affirmations of self-love:
I allow myself to love myself.

I am free to love who I am.
I am a special person; there is no one in the universe like me.
God loves me unconditionally.

Questioning how you really feel about a relationship:
I am open to my feelings.
I accept my feelings as truthful and real.
How do I truly feel about my relationship?

Seeking connection with another:
I am open to a growing relationship.
I allow myself the joys of a healthy relationship.

Seeking understanding of another:
I am open to the message being told me.
I am free to hear what is being said.
I seek honest and truthful communication.

Letting go of a relationship:
When I am ready, I am able to let go of this relationship with love.
I wish to move ahead, leaving this relationship with love.
I seek strength and growth for myself.

A second powerful technique in creating a reality of healthy relationships is *visualization*. This method augments dream incubation and, with practice, helps cut through emotional barriers that block understanding. Visualizations also inspire courage, giving us the added strength to behave differently in a relationship that will, in itself, initiate change. The technique is simple.

At bedtime, close your eyes and visualize yourself talking with your partner in a supportive, calm, loving atmosphere. *Ask what you would like to know, what you fear asking in waking reality.* Repeat this process as you fall asleep over the course of a week and listen to your dreams. Very often, what you hear may surprise you; but be prepared, dreams of relationships, as all dreams, are always truthful.

Incubation and visualization methods work by increasing *self-confidence, persistence, and commitment.* We draw upon inner strength that we were not previously aware of, find novel solutions that have escaped consciousness, adopt an open-minded attitude, reduce fear, break through emotional obstacles, and freely allow emotional healing to proceed without interference. Dreams of relationships are powerful tools in shaping waking reality.

My dreams create a reality of relationships when I increase awareness, incubate my dreams, and visualize for understanding, strength, and growth.

The Six Symbols of Relationships

- Communication
- Friendship
- Loneliness
- Love
- Need
- Sex

Symbols of Communication

Communication is an interpersonal exchange, allowing us to both *express* ourselves and *listen* to others, and forms the cornerstone of all relationships. Dreams of communication are valuable because they reveal the quality of our communication, which nearly always determines the character of our relationships.

These dreams may reflect *expressive* or *receptive* communication —how well we are able to verbalize our thoughts and feelings as well as listen to and learn from others. But because dreams of communication usually emerge when communication is strained, they are often accompanied by feelings of helplessness, tension, or frustration.

Expressive Communication

Expressive communication involves our ability to effectively express ourselves both verbally and nonverbally. Are we doing all that we can to clearly make our point or state our needs? Of course, no matter how eloquent, expression does not guarantee that others will *hear* what we are saying, but straightforward, unambiguous communication increases the chances of understanding.

Dreams of expressive communication appear when we feel frustrated with our attempts to express ourselves. Here are the three most common reasons why these dreams appear:

1. *Difficulty asking for what you want—making your needs known to someone.*

For most of us, asking for what we want is amazingly difficult. Sometimes the difficulty lies in our inability to be *clear* in our communication. When something is difficult to say, we often say it poorly. In my work with terminally ill patients, I have been struck by how poorly doctors provide this devastating prognosis to patients and families. In one instance a physician who tried to explain to the family that their father had little chance of surviving the night was so concerned with using euphemisms that the family had absolutely no idea what to expect of their father's condition following the conversation.

Clear, assertive, yet gentle communication without fear of reaction may seem intimidating but is usually best. Hinting at what you need rarely works, as no one can read your mind. Take responsibility for what you want by asking for it directly. If stubbornness or pride has kept you from expressing your feelings, put aside these unhelpful emotions, feel your fear, and then make your approach, gently and honestly.

2. *Trying to convince someone of your point of view.*

Though we don't like to admit it, we frequently seek to control others so that they'll see life from our point of view. Some dreams of communication reflect frustration—feeling unable to get your point across. However, the message you're trying to convey represents your own identity and reality at this time and is not necessarily the only way to look at the world. A surprisingly positive result may come from listening and truly hearing what another has to say.

3. *Regretting a hasty remark made while angry or irritated.*

Dreams of communication sometimes represent self-punishment, scolding yourself, particularly if your dream *feels* guilty. Guilt is useful if it appropriately tells us when to right a wrong, but don't be too harsh on yourself—uncaring remarks made impulsively rarely come from the heart. Do what you can to communicate your true feelings.

Receptive Communication

Receptive communication is more than listening, it is *hearing*. While this is perhaps our most important communication skill, it is also the most difficult to master. Fortunately, even when we don't consciously *hear*, the message being conveyed is processed unconsciously, and dreams can alert you to what you are missing.

Be attentive to these dream symbols; they are a signal that an important message has been overlooked:

◆ *Listening but not doing in a dream:*
  Consciously not hearing; ignoring
  Refusing to act on a message

◆ *Deafness or blindness:*
  Unable to *hear,* as the message is too psychologically overwhelming

◆ *Blank pages:*
  Not paying attention, too busy or preoccupied

◆ *Shouting or emphatic messages, such as huge writing:*
  Important message that you are refusing or unable to *hear*

◆ *Any dream that feels as if something is missing:*
  A message is too psychologically overwhelming
  Refusing to listen

Recurring Dreams

Dreams of communication often recur over weeks or months. They stubbornly persist at their task of alerting you that a relationship needs attention until you get the message. If you've had a dream of this sort before, then consider this is a consistent effort by your subconscious to create a state of awareness regarding your behavior, feelings, or a certain situation. Ask yourself the following questions:

◆ Am I truly listening?
◆ Am I allowing myself to hear?

- Is fear or something inside me preventing me from hearing?
- What important message is being communicated?

My dreams create a reality of relationships when I allow myself to listen without fear.

Symbols of Friendship

While nonromantic, nonsexual friendships are essential for personal growth and fulfillment, they are easily taken for granted. We assume that everyone has friends because everyone does know someone else. But being acquainted with someone and being a friend are not the same. Secure, trusting, and comfortable relationships are actually somewhat rare and are certainly wonderful.

Dreams of friendships may be the least common of all relationship dreams, but they are still important. They inform us about our friendship needs and the quality of our friend relationships and also seem to be related to safety and security issues.

Dreams of friendships emerge when we're stubbornly stoic, denying our need for friendship, pretending to ourselves that we can go it alone. No one can; what we sacrifice to be alone is far too great. We are naturally social creatures, and friendships are physically and psychologically beneficial—comfort from a good friend actually increases our immunity to disease, decreases emotional healing time, and reduces pain.

Dreams of friendships appear when we need a friend. They follow periods of loneliness and isolation or the need to confide in someone. If your friendship needs are not being met, expect to see these dreams emerge with some frequency.

As with any relationship, friendships require work; they don't just happen. Fortunately, since we all need friends, finding a friend is easier than it may seem. What usually prevents us from seeking new friendships is fear of rejection. However, what most of us don't realize is that the other person fears rejection just as much as we do.

To increase your self-confidence and strength in seeking new friendships, incubate your dreams of relationships with the following affirmations by repeating one quietly to yourself as you fall asleep:

I am free to explore new friendships.
I have much to offer, I am a desirable friend.
There are people who enjoy being with me.
I give myself permission to trust a friend.

Dreams of friendship also appear when friendships are troubled. If your dream felt unsettling or somehow unsafe, it may be alerting you to concerns about a friendship. Listen to your dreams and intuition—it's easy to dismiss these messages because they usually tell us something we *don't* want to hear.

Dreams of troubled friendships commonly appear for the following reasons:

+ Feeling unappreciated in a friendship
+ Inequity in a friendship, resentment, feeling taken advantage of
+ Concerns about trustworthiness
+ Feeling uncomfortably pressured by a friend in some way
+ Feeling unsafe or insecure in a friendship

My dreams create a reality of relationships when I allow myself to experience the comfort of good friendship.

Symbols of Loneliness

Loneliness is painful, especially so when we're recovering from the stinging loss that comes from ending an intimate relationship. Since feeling lonely is something we all experience from time to time, dreams of loneliness are not uncommon but come and go as friendships are lost or changed.

The most frequent dream symbols of loneliness include the following:

- Feelings and images of emptiness, abandonment, or isolation
- Dreams that feel lonely, self-doubting, anxious, but not agitated
- Images of withdrawal from social situations
- Hidden dream objects

Paradoxically, dreams of loneliness may also contain symbols of *crowds, parties, festivals, people,* and *images of the past, such as reliving joyous activities from a lost relationship.* This puzzling symbolism is a form of *dream compensation*—the unconscious, automatic, and natural healing process that occurs in our dreams in order to balance an emotional excess in waking reality.

Of course, dreams of loneliness emerge most frequently when we're feeling lonely. Most of us recognize this waking emotional state, although many avoid these unpleasant feelings by busying ourselves, becoming socially overinvolved, or spending time with people we really don't enjoy being with just to avoid being alone.

Dreams of loneliness may also appear when we feel lonely while in a relationship. When our needs are not being met, these dreams inform us as well as act as a pressure valve to safely isolate painful unexpressed emotions.

If you are repeatedly experiencing dreams of loneliness, ask yourself:

- Am I taking time for myself rather than being too busy?
- Am I avoiding being alone with myself?
- Am I hiding from loneliness?
- Am I socializing with people I don't really care for?
- Are my needs being met by my partner?

Symbols of Love

In former times there was a tradition where young maidens would put a handkerchief containing a peeled onion under their pillow for a vision of their lover in a dream. While few of us continue this practice, we still, of course, feel love in our dreams. However, dreams of love are usually subtle and rarely contain the actual image of our lovers. Instead the imagery tends to be more symbolic:

- Bells, jubilant sounds
- Calming ocean, beach, landscapes
- Cupid's arrow or other symbols you associate with love
- Joining, marriage
- New life or growth

Dreams of love *feel* loving, happy, content, serene, not melancholic. They are not loud but also not overly subdued; they seem to glow. They are pleasant, the kinds of dreams you don't want to wake from.

Dreams of love may also represent care and affection toward ourselves. This is *healthy selfishness,* positive and psychologically beneficial, and associated with peace, joy, and success.

My dreams create a reality of relationships when I love myself unconditionally.

Wish Fulfillment

Classic psychoanalysis teaches that dreams safely fulfill wishes not attainable in waking reality. If you want something that's not available to you—a lover, money, power, even a vacation—dreams create a fantasy where these wishes are satisfied. There seems to be some truth to this in the sense that we frequently have fanciful wishes in our dreams.

Dreams of love, then, may be *wishing* for love. Such dream symbolism is usually clear and undisguised:

- ◆ Wedding
- ◆ Bride, bridegroom
- ◆ Honeymoon

Wish fulfillment is a natural process and is based on the concept of *balance;* what we lack in waking reality is compensated for in our dreams.

Symbols of Need

Humans need one another. Of course, infants are completely dependent upon their parents for all of their *physical* needs such as food and shelter, but what tends to be unspoken in our society is that babies are *emotionally* dependent as well. Small children still must be nurtured, and adolescence is the awkward process of learning to balance one's psychological needs with those of another. As adults we seek a partner, someone who fits us, who supplies us with what we cannot, a complement to our strengths and weaknesses. We have friends to share our struggles and triumphs, to listen, to care, to exchange energy.

That we *need* others in this way is not a popular belief in this current age of independence. We would rather believe that as individuals we are wholly and totally complete within ourselves and that relationships are merely a matter of choice, nice but not necessary. It is far easier and less risky to depend only on oneself—however, few of us can truly grow in emotional isolation.

Dreams of need are *selfish* and concern themselves only with what is emotionally lacking in *our* life. They are *egocentric,* meaning that they center around our ego and, without hesitation, discard the needs and feelings of others.

This may seem coldhearted, even cruel, but it is not. Each one of us needs to take care of our self before we can properly take care of anyone else. We need to love ourselves before we can love or be loved, be kind to ourselves before we can truly be kind to others.

Furthermore, dreams are never selfish at the expense of others but have the *innocent selfishness* of small children. Children see the world only from their own perspective and cannot understand when others do not see things as they do. Having their needs met is all that's important, regardless of how inconvenient or even impossible this is for their caregivers. But we certainly do not call small children unkind or uncaring; this is their nature. This is also the nature of our dreams of need.

Feeling Needy

While all of us search for human connection, our desire for companionship differs. Feeling *needy* in a dream is a sign that our emotional needs, whatever they may be, are not being met. Just as our need for food is signaled by hunger, dream neediness tells us what is necessary for emotional survival.

Dreams of need feel needy. They signal emotional hunger, difficult to describe but easily felt. Take a moment, think back, and *feel* your dream:

- Does it feel as if something is lacking?
- Do you have a sense of longing?
- Are you searching for something?
- Do you notice a yearning for human connection or touch?
- Is there something missing in this dream?

This symbolism tells you of needs not met in your waking life. They are relationship based and may be associated with intimate, parent-child, friend, or even professional interactions.

The Joy of Relationships

It's been said that there is no hope of joy except in human relationships. Certainly our connection to others—spouse, partner, friend, parent, child—is among the greatest joys we will experience in life; this is why dreams of relationships can be so powerful.

Use your dreams of need to help search out what you are lacking, what your emotional needs are—being prepared that this search will take determination, strength, and courage.

> My dreams create a reality of relationships when I listen
> courageously for my true needs.

Symbols of Sex

Sexual dreams, while seldom mentioned, are among the most common of all. The famous *Kinsey* studies found that these dreams occur in all ages, in both genders, and regardless of attitudes about sex.

But for many, sexual dreams dismay, even repulse. Two hundred years ago we believed that these dreams caused mental illness, and before that we thought them inspired by demons. In the Middle Ages sexual dreams were considered the work of *Incubus* and *Succubus*. Incubus, a male demon, and Succubus, a female demon, roamed the earth at night and, for pleasure, tormented sleepers. It was believed that these demons sat on your chest as you slept and, with their face close to yours, fiendishly watched you breathe. They might play by strangling you, creating dreams of suffocation, but what they enjoyed most was having sex with you, creating, as you might guess, sexual dreams.

Even today, sexual dreams are a great source of guilt for many. We are a sexually immature society—fascinated and titillated with sex but refusing openly to admit it. We skirt the limits of what is acceptable in the media, condemn on one hand and peek on the other. However, sexuality is a crucial part of ourselves that we need to recognize and accept.

Sexual dreams are always honest. They are about us, we create them, and they recognize our needs, no matter how primitive they may seem. Look to your sexual dreams for

- a healthy, safe release of sexual tensions.
- information about your sexual needs and desires.
- a barometer of your intimate relationships.
- a source of great pleasure.

Sexual dreams are sometimes a glimpse at the more primitive elements of our psyche—our sexual or aggressive instincts and unconscious desires. In Freudian terms this is our id—the part of our psyche that attempts to experience what is unacceptable in waking reality. This is a perfectly natural, healthy, and safe process, often a release of sexual energies. However, many people, particularly those of us who have a strong need for control, find sexual dreams disconcerting, embarrassing, or threatening.

But remember that dreams aren't meant to embarrass or threaten you in any way. Sexual dreams can be a glimpse of your untamed subconscious and provide for safe expression of natural human impulses.

Ironically, the more we try to suppress sexual feelings and desires in waking life, the more powerfully they emerge in dreams. Too much suppression yields wildly sexual dreams that, to be ignored, must be consciously blocked.

Sexual Dreams Are an Intimate Look at Our Closest Relationships

Sexual dreams inform us about the quality of our intimate and sexual relationships. As is always the case, imagery is less important than the feeling in interpreting these dreams. It doesn't matter *who* you are having sex with in a dream; don't feel guilty or embarrassed if it is not your regular partner. In fact, dreams of actually making love to our partners are rare. Instead, *feel* your dreams—sexual dreams suggestive of relationship or sexual concerns have a distinctive feel. Here are some common themes:

• *If you're uncomfortable with your sexual partner:*
   Sex without intimacy
   Sex without feeling—just going through the motions
   Unpleasant or painful sex

• *If conflict in a relationship is interfering with sexual satisfaction:*
   Unsatisfying sex in dreams
   Unarousing sexual dreams
   Sex without intimacy
   Distinctly nonerotic and unarousing, but sex as a duty or
      chore

* *Feeling guilty about sex:*
    Disgusting or offensive feelings
    Excessively erotic dreams—feels like too much
    Unarousing sexual dreams
    Dreams of sexual dysfunction

* *If your sexual needs are not being met:*
    Dreams with excessive sexual imagery and feelings
    Feeling jealous in a sexual dream

* *Wishing for something different or more adventurous sexuality:*
    Very erotic dreams, including sexual fantasies
    Dreams of sexual activities that you have never tried
    Pornography or prostitution in dreams

* *When you're too inhibited to ask for what you really want:*
    Very erotic dreams, including sexual fantasies
    Excessively erotic dreams

Sexual dreams can be a source of great pleasure. Remember they are a creation of your unconscious mind, and there is nothing unhealthy, abnormal, or obscene about these dreams. Leave the guilt behind; these very private experiences are yours alone to enjoy.

My dreams create a reality of relationships when I learn to accept my sexual dreams as normal, healthy, and natural.

CHAPTER FOUR

Dreaming for Prosperity

∼ Dreams of prosperity are among the most common yet perhaps the most misunderstood dreams that we experience. The frequency of these dreams should come as no surprise, as dreaming reflects waking concerns and prosperity is of great interest to us all. These dreams are misunderstood because we neglect them—we ignore their vitality to empower us to achieve what we desire in life.

Dreaming for prosperity is acknowledging the power of dreams to create a reality of personal fulfillment, satisfying our needs and wants.

How Can I Recognize My Dreams of Prosperity?

Prosperity is defined as *having success or flourishing*. It is about material success, but it is also much more. It is creating achievement, personal fulfillment, satisfaction, contentment, security. Prosperity is to money as spirituality is to religion: spirituality is boundless, religion is one simple expression of the infinite spirit. Likewise, prosperity goes well beyond work and finances. It includes these, but it is also creating a sense of purpose by excellence in accomplishment in one's chosen roles. By this definition, then, we can work and make enormous amounts of money *without* being prosperous.

Dreams of prosperity willingly reveal themselves once we know what to look for. However, we usually miss them or they seem without meaning because most of us don't think of dreaming as a vehicle for increasing prosperity. They don't address what we commonly expect from our dream analysis—psychological problems, health concerns, or relationship issues. They tend to feel bland, mundane, and blend into the morass of consciousness, where they're easily discarded.

But if we make a conscious effort to attend to these dreams and to create a reality of prosperity, we are given a map that clearly and directly guides us to their meaning.

Dreams of prosperity inform us of our beliefs, attitudes, prejudices, and emotional reactions to success, and they guide in creating a reality of prosperity.

These dreams observe and create prosperity simultaneously—a concept that may at first seem difficult to comprehend. We often discuss these two facets of dreaming—reflecting reality and creating reality—separately in order to simplify them. But it is the fundamental nature of dreams as well as all reality that observation is invasive. Dreaming cannot observe without altering.

From subatomic particles to human interaction, watching something changes it. Observing an electron alters its path, and anyone who has started a diet just by *watching* what they eat knows that this self-monitoring alone induces some behavior change. In science, this invasive effect of observation is known as the *Heisenberg principle*. Since most of us wish to *increase* our prosperity, the Heisenberg principle is, in this case, a welcome side effect.

We begin the process of change as soon as we acknowledge the power of dreams to create a reality of prosperity. Look for subtle imagery and emotional themes to reflect dreams of prosperity. Generally, symbols of prosperity are characterized by the following:

+ Any symbols of achievement, accomplishment, or success
+ Money
+ Symbols of wealth such as precious metals, jewels, priceless objects
+ Symbolism involving giving as well as receiving
+ Travel to a specific and clear destination

Dreams of prosperity may take the forms of work, money, ambition, achievement, personal fulfillment, and security.

Work

Work is the most visible sign of our pursuit of prosperity. We, of course, work for income but derive social status, professional identity, and other benefits as well. However, while we spend the majority of our waking hours at work, many of us find little satisfaction and lack a sense of fulfillment with our job. This is impoverishing at a deep level. Common sense alone suggests we seek meaning in anything we spend such a great amount of time at. Dreaming for prosperity informs us of our need to seek purpose in our work and to acknowledge the value and meaning of everyday efforts.

Symbols of work are sometimes represented by a dream character's occupation or the imagery of someone working. How you perceive the status of this dreamed occupation is believed to represent your opinions about *your* profession.

Money

Money is one of the most dominating forces on the planet. It has become imbued with such power through its constant association with primary reinforcers: food, water, sex. In fact, although not biologically programmed (we are not born to seek money as we do food and water), money has become a *functional primary reinforcer*—it *is* food and water, as well as all material goods.

By itself, of course, money is meaningless. It is merely paper fiber and metal alloys, but its mystique and artificially limited supply creates power. No matter how much we have, we seem to *need* more—there are few millionaires who do not strive to increase their fortune.

Money is also misunderstood. It is not the root of all evil, it does not solve personal problems, and it is not the measure of one's value. But how you view money—your personal myths, fears, and prejudices—will be reflected in your dreams. If you believe that money, or the lack of it, is the source of all problems in your life, you will dream of money as both an evil and a solution. However, your dreams will be shallow—dream money may flow, but dream solutions will remain elusive. As in waking reality, money by itself is never a solution—it merely exchanges one set of problems for another.

Dreams of money are readily apparent and usually symbolized by the following:

- Paper currency, coins, credit cards
- Checks, investments, bonds, stocks, financial portfolios
- Miser, beggar
- Wages, salary
- Debt, irresponsible spending
- Banks and other financial institutions
- Buying your way into something

Use the *feel* of your dream within the context of waking reality to interpret this symbolism. Money concerns are usually conscious and no mystery, but if you're uncertain, ask yourself these questions:

- Are my spending habits too extravagant?
- Is money a chronic worry? If so, are these concerns realistic or a result of conditioning?
- Am I in a position to potentially lose a great deal of money?
- Am I obsessed with money?
- Is my self-image tied to my net worth?

Ambition

Ambition, *a desire for prosperity,* is symbolized in dreams. People we refer to as *dreamers,* those who live by their hopes and aspirations, realistic or not, frequently experience these dreams of prosperity. Some ambitious individuals act on their desires; others do not—either way these feelings surface in dreams. Common dream symbols include the following:

- Maps, sometimes fictitious treasure maps
- Stars, sky, celestial bodies
- Astrology, prediction, fortune-telling, particularly as these divinations apply to wealth

Achievement

Dreaming for prosperity creates achievement. It gives us the strength and perseverance to successfully accomplish our goals by empowering us, removing psychological obstacles, dissipating fear and doubt, seeding expectations of success, and focusing our energy on the task.

We experience these dreams both when we're successful and when we're struggling. They are part of the reward of accomplishment as well as a guide to overcoming the emotional obstacles that hinder progress. *But most important, dreaming for prosperity melts away doubts that impede success.* Symbols of achievement are not disguised but can be easily overlooked:

- Fame, notoriety
- Prizes, awards, medals
- Educational degrees, graduation
- Halo—great achievements
- Agricultural harvest—the seeds of prosperity have come to fruition

Personal Fulfillment

Dreaming for prosperity reflects great joy and satisfaction. When we are successful we have the unique opportunity to feel a heightened sense of purpose, empowerment, and personal fulfillment. Any task well done is a success whether or not it has perceived social value or importance. A child successfully scrawling her first letters on a page is as personally valuable and fulfilling as is making a million dollars. Dreaming for prosperity restores this sense of priorities by teaching us to recognize what is truly important and to acknowledge that social values are sometimes misleading and superficial.

Dream symbols of personal fulfillment are typically emotional rather than visual:

- A dream that feels fulfilling
- A sense of deep satisfaction, purpose, or importance
- Birth, new life that feels wondrous
- Smooth, flowing, calming water—spiritual fulfillment

Security

Dreaming for prosperity increases our sense of security. This is not limited to financial security based upon bank statements and net worth, but is a sense of *personal* security even in the face of uncertainty. It is a willingness to accept that solutions emerge in unpredictable ways and that uncertainty is, paradoxically, a form of security.

It's been said that to acquire something one must first relinquish attachment to it. This is a difficult concept to grasp, particularly for those of us constantly in a *state of want*—conditioned from a very young age by television and other media to *need* material goods. But when we refuse to relinquish attachment to objects, their nonattainment, loss, or potential loss becomes a great source of insecurity.

However, this state of want and therefore insecurity exists only in waking reality, not in dream reality. Dream reality is pure; our unconscious mind is not swayed by shallow advertisements or slogans. Its priorities are correct; it knows what we need and that we can attain these needs. Dreaming for prosperity creates security by defining and ordering our priorities. It fleshes out what is real and substantive from what is illusion.

Dreams of security usually feel safe and comfortable and may include symbolism such as a secure, warm, and solid house. Symbols of *insecurity*, on the other hand, usually feel insecure and are readily apparent:

+ Locks, doors, guards
+ Fixed retirement money such as pensions, retirement funds
+ Feeling insecure

What Will I Learn from My Dreams of Prosperity?

Dreams of prosperity are frequent and informative. If you listen, you will learn a great deal about yourself—how you face money and achievement issues. Look for subtleties in your dreams, remembering that these dreams are sometimes difficult to *feel* because the feelings are not pronounced. But as you create a reality of prosperity through dreams, the symbolism becomes clearer. Here are some commonly experienced *waking realities* together with likely dream symbolism:

Money Dreams

+ *Money is too important:*
    Frequent money symbols; frantic over losing money

+ *Seeking wealth without responsibility:*
    Careless spending; observing poverty in others without
    concern; huge amounts of wealth but void of satisfaction

+ *Realistic concerns about money:*
    Feelings of dread associated with any dream money symbols

+ *Obsession or excessive worry about money:*
    Frequent money dreams; finding and hoarding coins

Achievement Dreams

+ *If too much of your self-worth is based on success:*
    Successful theatrical or other public performances; others in
    adoration over dream character's accomplishments

+ *If you need money or success to feel powerful:*
    Hoarding money; overly protecting wealth; strong but lonely
    or isolated dream characters

+ *A lack of fulfillment in your work:*
    Boredom or dread associated with work symbols

+ *Emotional or psychological obstacles to achievement:*
    Walls, barriers; feels like a dream of self-understanding with
    helplessness, frustration

Security Dreams

+ *Excessive fear, doubt, or insecurity:*
    Dreams *feel* anxious or insecure regardless of imagery

+ *Expectations for success:*
    Clear goal or destination of travel; feeling of strength,
    optimism without doubt

+ *Expectations for failure:*
  Outcomes that are sabotaged; work without end or results; doubt

How Do I Incubate My Dreams of Prosperity?

Learning from our dreams of prosperity also means learning to incubate these dreams for guidance. *Incubation* is the process of seeding the unconscious to grow a desired outcome—posing a question, presenting a problem, asking for clarification, expressing a desire. Remember, dreams are dynamic; they respond to our conscious intent as well as shape it. We can learn to exercise a great deal of control over waking reality as we become more adept at creating a powerful dream reality.

Dream guidance is profound because it flows from the unlimited resources of the unconscious mind. Of course, our unconscious is aware of every bit of us—our physiology and behavior, our deepest thoughts, feelings, and desires—but this part of the mind is also connected to all life through the *collective* and *spiritual* unconscious (see chapter 5). It is unbounded by our individualism and draws from the knowledge and energy of the universe as well as from the strength of all living things.

While we are consciously aware of only the smallest portion of this potential, we can still harness its power by directing our needs and desires beyond the confines of our separateness, a process most easily attained though dream incubation.

Dream incubation is a simple process. At bedtime form your question or request as an affirmation and repeat it quietly to yourself as you fall asleep. Keep your affirmations short and direct, and pose only a single question at a time. For instance:

I allow myself to recognize the best path for my business actions.
I am willing to accept success.
I choose to increase my awareness of prosperity.
I seek fulfillment in all my professional endeavors.
I allow myself to hear what my dreams are telling me.

Learning from dreams of prosperity also means learning to connect dream reality with the success and defeats of waking life. Our dreams reflect what concerns us most, supplying clear honest feedback unaffected by the emotional clutter and psychological defenses of waking reality. If we are worried about money or a professional matter, dreaming will tell us why and what to do about it. If rigid thinking or prejudiced attitudes impede success, our dreams will inform us. Connect dream and waking realities in these four ways:

1. Listen to your dream; feel its reality.
2. Think about which specific events in your life may relate your dream feelings.
3. Look for recurring dreams—those with similar themes but perhaps dissimilar imagery.
4. Avoid judgment—keep an open mind to what your dream may be saying, remembering that you are seeking guidance because your waking point of view is imperfect.

Be prepared to discover that your most fervently held belief is not the truth it seems and for your unconscious to enlighten you as to how this belief has been holding you back. This discrepancy between dream and waking realities is more common than most of us realize; the classic example is dreams that provide insight into behavior and attitudes that sabotage success when we're afraid of succeeding.

My dreams create a reality of prosperity when I connect my unconscious wisdom with my conscious behavior.

How Can My Dreams Create a Reality of Prosperity?

There is an age-old wisdom threaded through the beliefs of many cultures that prosperity is our natural state of being. We tend to overlook this in our society because we see so many who do not prosper either financially or spiritually. We also forget what it means to prosper, thinking mistakenly that money by itself creates happiness, contentment, and security. But if we accept that prosperity is the *perfect balance of giving and receiving,* then we see that this indeed is our natural state, as balance is a fundamental law of the universe.

If we seek only to receive and not to give, then we will never prosper. If we seek success at the expense of others, our achievements will be hollow and temporary. But if we *balance* our lives with equal parts of giving and receiving, then prosperity is boundless.

My dreams create a reality of prosperity when I accept that prosperity is my natural state—the state of perfect balance of giving and receiving.

Every culture takes a different path to attain prosperity. In the West we focus on effort and hard work—we tackle problems head on, work long hours, find value in competition, and are obsessed with productivity. *Work hard and get ahead,* or, *There is no success without hardship*—these define the path to prosperity.

New Age philosophers and Vedic beliefs stress a path of least resistance—a spiritual approach where connecting to the Infinite through intention and desire creates a reality of prosperity. The mechanics of this process include learning to just *be* through meditation, silence, and nonjudgment.

These two paths seem quite separate, but fundamentally both seek prosperity through equilibrium—the harmonious, stable state of being in which the universe rests.

Regardless of your personal beliefs and the path you choose, your dreams will create a reality of prosperity by

- giving you the information and guidance you need to make confident choices.
- helping you to honestly evaluate your needs and desires.
- teaching you how to creatively approach intransigent problems.
- empowering you by transcending doubt, negativity, and emotional obstacles.

- inspiring creativity.
- generating energy and perseverance.

Empowering Choice

Dreaming for prosperity creates better decisions. They are *better* in that decision making becomes more automatic—there is less doubt, less apprehension, less regret. Dreaming supplies self-assurance—the recognition that there is no wrong choice, only the best choice for the moment. We learn that hindsight is an illusion—no matter how compelling it may seem, we *cannot* know what our world would be like if only we'd made a different choice.

Dreaming for prosperity provides direction and guidance in our decisions. It puts us in touch with our innermost feelings, balances our rational and intuitive sides, and releases emotional blocks. This process is automatic; there is nothing you need to do to make it happen. Once you accept that your dreams will create a reality of prosperity, choices become more spontaneous and less tentative.

My dreams create a reality of prosperity when I accept that hindsight is an illusion and that I make the best choices possible at the moment.

You can also incubate your dreams for guidance with specific decisions. Use the same basic incubation procedure just described, repeating affirmations for guidance with whatever decision you are facing:

I allow myself to explore the possibilities for this decision.
I allow myself to find a solution.
I am open to guidance for my choice.

Honestly Evaluate Your Needs and Desires

It's unfortunate, but many of us, if we believed that we had the choice, would opt for work other than our occupation. Still others deny their true feelings, convincing themselves that they find fulfillment in a job when they do not. This conscious or latent dissatisfaction is a source of deep hurt, stress, lost energy, and lost productivity and a prescription for the defeat of prosperity.

Dreaming for prosperity keeps us in touch with our *true* feelings —but be prepared for a dream's brutal honesty, as it will tell you the truth even if this is not what you want to hear. These are common symbols of need and desire associated with work:

• *Sabotaging your own efforts:*
    Outcomes that are sabotaged
    Work without end or results
    Doubt

• *Denial of true attitudes toward your work:*
    Boredom or dread associated with work symbols

There is an old adage that perhaps best defines dreaming for prosperity: *Do what you love, and the money will follow.*

Facilitating Creative Problem Solving

Creating a reality of prosperity almost always involves being challenged to find solutions. Fortunately it has long been known that dreams solve problems by furnishing different points of view, painting a clearer perspective, and allowing us to get unstuck in our thinking. And because we can view situations differently in a dream, solutions that have eluded conscious awareness often become accessible.

You can incubate for solutions to specific problems by posing your question in the form of a simple, direct affirmation, repeating it quietly to yourself while falling asleep. Adopt an attitude of *detachment* —that is, allow this problem to become *less* significant; no matter how important it seems, a solution will come in its own time. Obsessive worry always inhibits problem solving—it's a paradox, but as the importance you attach to a problem fades, its solution becomes clearer.

My dreams create a reality of prosperity by guiding solutions to problems that elude conscious awareness.

Transcending Doubt, Negativity, and Emotional Obstacles

Doubt and negativity are our greatest challenges to creating a reality of prosperity. These barriers are insidious; they build gradually, almost invisibly, slowly draining away physical energy and psychological resources. They seed worry, fear, and self-consciousness, deflate ambition, and sabotage success.

Doubt and negativity in a dream are usually clear and unambiguous—a dream plainly *feels* negative. What follows are *common symbols of doubt and negativity.*

+ *Fear of failure:*
  Feeling overwhelmed, confused
  Poor communication of any sort
  Feeling weak—no energy
  Unreasonably cautious, taking the safe route even with low
    risk
  No matter how much work a dream character does, nothing
    seems to get accomplished

+ *Negativity and a chronic need to complain:*
  Gossip in a dream
  Witnessing failure or a desire to see others fail

+ *Overly aggressive attitude, always ready for a fight:*
  Aggressive, hostile dream figures
  Feelings of anger, hostility, frustration, fear
  Feeling discouraged, irritable—a short fuse
  Risky, irresponsible behavior

+ *Tendency to quit too soon:*
  Unreasonably cautious, taking the safe route even with low
    risk
  Low energy, depression
  Feeling guilty
  The end is in sight, but it's never reached

- *Emotional turmoil that prevents prosperity:*
    Dimmed awareness—nothing is clear, everything seems
        fuzzy
    Feeling confused
    Dream characters who are unable to concentrate
    Feeling weak—no energy or absorbed in an emotional
        problem
    Work in a dream is unproductive; nothing seems to get done

Creative Dreaming

Dreaming for prosperity empowers your creative resources in a way not possible during waking reality. You are not bound by the restraints of reason and logic, but are free to consider alternatives that otherwise might be overlooked. Creative thinking has long been associated with dreaming, and there are many fascinating examples of scientific and artistic achievements inspired by dreams.

- *Einstein's dream:*
    Albert Einstein is said to have dreamed of flying a sled
    through the heavens, accelerating faster and faster until,
    when he reached the speed of light, the stars began to
    change into spectacular shapes and colors. Einstein claimed
    that the inspiration for his theory of relativity came from
    this dream.

- *Jack Nicklaus's dream:*
    Professional golfer Jack Nicklaus believes he improved his
    golf game by ten strokes because of a new way to grip the
    club—a method he learned from a dream.

- *Descartes's dream:*
    Seventeenth-century philosopher René Descartes is said to
    have dreamed the basic concepts for the system of
    mathematics that we use today.

- *Robert Louis Stevenson's dream:*
    This author derived the plot for his book *Dr. Jekyll and
    Mr. Hyde* from a dream.

+ *Joseph Smith's dream:*
It's said that the founder of the Mormon Church had a
dream vision in which he found plates of gold. He later went
to the location of his dream and reportedly discovered these
gold plates inscribed with the teachings of the Mormon
religion.

Creative dreaming is one of the easiest ways to become comfortable with the incubation process. At bedtime program your dreams to provide novel solutions for specific problems. Consider these affirmations:

I allow myself to see this situation from different perspectives.
I am free to explore new ideas and perspectives.
I release any need to judge or evaluate.

When you wake let your ideas flow—*brainstorm,* don't evaluate or judge, and you'll be surprised by the wonderfully eclectic nature of your creative dreaming.

Generating Energy and Perseverance

Dreaming for prosperity creates energy. We feel empowered to undertake tasks that we might otherwise shy away from, put more intellectual and psychological resources into our work, expand our creative horizons, and, most important, *persevere.*

There is an abundance of evidence that perseverance leads to success. We've all heard scores of stories of ambitious individuals who have endured countless setbacks on the road to their accomplishments. Unfortunately, most of us faced with the stark reality of our own circumstances say to ourselves, "That may have happened to them, but that's not me." This is a perfect example of how waking reality sabotages ambition.

Dreams don't give up. If your desire is real and responsible, then your dream will empower you with the energy necessary to keep going and face adversity with courage and optimism. Watch for recurrent dream symbols of hope, strength, and courage. Incubate your dreams with affirmations such as the following:

I create my reality of prosperity through the power of my dreams.
I affirm my desire and release my need for an outcome.
I flow with the natural order, allowing prosperity to engulf me.
I pass on my prosperity.
I allow myself to realize my true ambitions.
I am responsible in my desires.
I am aware of my needs and desires, but not obsessed by them.
I follow sensible actions and beliefs.

The Six Symbols of Prosperity

+ Choice
+ Energy
+ Intellect
+ Opportunity
+ Wealth
+ Work

Symbols of Choice

Choice often feels paralyzing, as if you are standing on a precipice, frozen, undecided, knowing you must move but not knowing how, resulting in an erosion of your sense of self-confidence. Perhaps this is why *valleys* or *canyons* in dreams often symbolize choice—and your perception of the seriousness of a decision is represented by the depth of the dream image.

Difficult decisions paralyze us because we fear making the wrong choice. *But in reality, there is no wrong choice*—since we have infinite choices, we have only one—the one that we choose is the only one we are *able* to choose at the time. As soon as we choose, all others melt away, and their subsequent realities no longer exist. Hindsight is an illusion—no matter how compelling it may seem, we *cannot* know what our world would be like if only we'd made a different choice. That different choice does not exist, never has, and never will.

Dreaming for prosperity allows us to use all of our resources to investigate alternatives. Waking reason, analysis, and common sense all play a significant and useful role—ignoring them and basing choices solely on spiritual attunement is never wise. This is just another form of imbalance, as misleading as purely rational, unintuitive, nonspiritual thinking. Right brain and left brain were meant to check and balance one another.

If you have a tendency toward imbalance, such as being biased in favor of intuition over reason, your dreams of prosperity will tell you. Look for these symbols of imbalance:

+ Dream objects that are out of proportion, overly large or small
+ Distances that seem to stretch
+ Lopsided images—for example, an unevenly weighted scale
+ Obviously unfair play
+ Music out of harmony

When our decisions are imbalanced, based on thinking that's too rational or behavior that's too impulsive, dreams of prosperity inform us.

My dreams create a reality of prosperity when I allow myself to balance intuition with reason in decision making.

Creative Dreaming

Dreaming for prosperity empowers your creative resources, allowing you to consider alternatives that otherwise may be overlooked. Creative thinking has long been associated with dreaming, and as I discussed earlier, there are a multitude of examples of successful ideas inspired by dreams. Creative dreaming is also one of the easiest ways to become comfortable with the incubation process. At bedtime program your dreams to provide novel solutions using creativity affirmations such as these:

I allow myself to see this situation from different perspectives.
I am free to explore new ideas and perspectives.
I release any need to judge or evaluate.

Dream symbols associated with travel also represent choice. Metaphorically you're at a decision point—ready to travel but needing to make a choice regarding your ultimate direction and destination. As always, the emotional tone of your dream holds insight into your true feelings about this new venture.

Draw upon your resources, investigate alternatives, spend some reflective quiet time, and then move forward with your choice. Accept that this decision is the best and therefore the *only* one that you are able to make at the time.

Symbols of Energy

Energy, both physical and psychic, is the driving force that powers ambition and achievement. However, we tend to take personal energy for granted, thinking little of it until we lose it to physical fatigue or emotional listlessness.

The *first law of thermodynamics* states that energy can be neither created nor destroyed but merely interchanged. This means that physical and psychic energy will always manifest in some way—constructively if channeled in a creative, thoughtful manner, or destructively if not harnessed. Dreams of energy remind us that we control this process; it's up to us whether or not our energy is used productively.

Dreams of energy represent the physical and psychic energy necessary to obtain prosperity. Energy symbols come in many forms:

- Fire, fuel, or burning
- Food
- Mechanical energy such as engines or machines
- Natural energy such as a volcano
- Symbols of personal strength such as bravery or physical musculature
- Atomic energy
- Man-made heat such as a furnace
- Electricity
- Certain dreams of exercise and other strenuous physical activities

Fire

Symbols of fire are among the most common dreams of energy. They may refer to physical or emotional energy particularly, as these relate to ambition and achievement. While each dream and dreamer is unique, there are a number of likely interpretations for dreams of fire.

+ *Destruction associated with fire:*
    A change in mind-set or attitude that can affect prosperity
    A signal to channel your creative energies constructively

+ *Fire symbols in a dream that feels sexually arousing:*
    Dreams of energy often have sexual overtones; consider
        whether your sexual needs are being met

+ *Fire associated with restless energy:*
    A burning desire or aspiration creating tension
    Need for physical release

+ *Starting a fire:*
    A sign of new beginnings or a new project

+ *A flame that won't extinguish:*
    Focused mental and creative energies
    Determination that often results in success
    Obsession

+ *Harm or injury from a fire or energy symbol:*
    Ambivalence to undertake a new project

+ *Weak energy symbolism—for example, a fire struggling to burn:*
    Low psychic, physical, or sexual energy
    A signal not to get sidetracked by unimportant details
    Center yourself, focus your energies, and assume
        responsibility

+ *Smoldering fire:*
    Holding on to old attitudes simply because they're familiar
    Unfocused or restless energy

Strength

Dreams of energy often symbolize *personal strength*. This may refer to anything from ambitious creative plans to the simple energy it takes to accomplish daily chores. Themes such as bravery, courage, or toughness refer to your ability to *focus* your energy— is it powerful and productive, or has it become an emotional and physical drain? The *feeling* of your dream is most telling in interpreting this symbolism, as strength imagery is sometimes paradoxical.

+ *Symbols of bravery and courage that feel strong:*
  Ambition
  A single-minded sense of purpose
  Idealism embodying your hopes and dreams for the future
  Growth by stretching your abilities
  Confidence

+ *Paradoxical symbols of bravery and courage, ones that feel weak:*
  Difficulty getting day-to-day tasks accomplished
  A signal to reenergize and assert control over unfinished
    business
  Focus on neglected but necessary matters
  Pay greater attention to detail

Symbols of Intellect

Dreams of the intellect represent the power of logic and reason —*left-brain thinking* that characterizes analyzing, problem solving, weighing alternatives, or calculating. This is commonsense thinking that obeys the rules of waking reality.

Intellect should never be underestimated—it is the power that created our physical infrastructure, the modern technology that we now take for granted. *It is the language of mathematics and science, and it has irrevocably shaped our world.*

Intellect is an extremely valuable resource, but it is also as seductive as a siren. Because of our great scientific achievements, we are tempted to believe that intellect will eventually solve all problems, that it gives us a kind of omnipotence and sets us apart from other species. We become reductionists—*everything* can ultimately be broken down into its components and explained by technology.

This position is as naive as it is arrogant. It is false because it contradicts the most basic tenet of the universe—*the law of balance.* Intellect is always balanced by intuition, and dreams of intellect are sometimes a paradox, warning that we've slipped out of harmony, relying too much on reason or being overly intuitive. It seems to be a human tendency to polarize, shifting between extremes of left brain and right brain; dreams of intellect inform us of this imbalance.

My dreams create a reality of prosperity when I balance intellect and intuition.

Dreams of Knives and Other Sharp Objects

Dream symbols of knives or other sharp instruments are common expressions of intellect. These represent reason, intellectual sharpness, the ability to cut to the real issue. They also warn not to cut away feelings and that intellect without intuition is misguided; it is the difference between knowledge and wisdom.

Dreaming of a sharp object used constructively symbolizes intellectual sharpness and sound reasoning. But a sharp instrument wielded irresponsibly indicates that you're getting bogged down—that it's time to examine your priorities and cut through the numerous time-consuming tasks that impede progress and prevent real achievement.

A sharp object being wielded in a *threatening* manner symbolizes a desire for retribution—to get even for a perceived injustice. You may be feeling angry, perhaps cheated; ask yourself if you have an ax to grind.

Symbols of intellect are often associated with waking stress. This is because the circumstances that precipitate these dreams are typically challenging emotionally and physically. It's not unusual, then, for dreams of intellect to be accompanied by symbols of anxiety and tension.

> My dreams create a reality of prosperity as I accept responsibility for my decisions and actions.

Symbols of Opportunity

Symbols of opportunity are powerful dreams of prosperity in that they often reveal opportunities that waking consciousness overlooks. Dreams of opportunity enable us to see the hidden potential—to recognize a diamond in the rough.

> My dreams create a reality of prosperity when I listen for opportunity.

Doors, walls, dams, and other dream symbols of obstruction may appear to be barriers but in reality represent *opportunity*. It's been said that the pessimist sees difficulty in every opportunity while the optimist sees opportunity in every difficulty; dreams of opportunity empower us with optimism.

The circumstances that precipitate these dreams vary; to interpret them, first ask yourself a few questions:

- Have I noticed myself shying away from doing something new, listing countless reasons why I shouldn't when in fact I'm losing opportunities because of fear?
- Do I usually go it alone, keeping others at a safe distance, defensive about my plans?
- Have I refused offers because they meant sharing the rewards with others?
- Am I afraid to fail?

There are riches in every opportunity even when we fail—and seeing opportunity only as difficulty stifles achievement. Dreams of opportunity teach that failure is an invaluable lesson and that every accomplishment is built on a mountain of disappointments. *Open yourself to opportunity, even the opportunity to fail.*

Failure is frightening only when we become too attached to a particular outcome. If we believe that only a certain set of events, a particular way of being—accumulating great wealth, for instance—is *necessary* for prosperity, then we have become too attached to this result; fear of *not* achieving leads to obsession.

Instead, practice detaching from the outcome. *Detachment* is the Vedic paradox of relinquishing attachment to any result and separating your sense of self from this result. Most of us find this a difficult concept to accept, but it is a powerful one.

Detach in your dreams. Create a reality of detachment by affirming your desire, affirming your intention, but letting go of the result. Remember that prosperity is our natural state, and like a river, it will flow if its path is not blocked. Use these affirmations to incubate your dreams of opportunity:

I am aware of, but not obsessed with, my intentions and desires.
I detach from any outcome.
I affirm my desires, allowing them to create my reality.

Symbols of Wealth

Dreams of wealth are the most common prosperity dreams and usually appear as images of money, gems, or precious metals. Less frequently they include other financial symbols such as stocks and bonds or buried treasure or more latent symbolism such as elaborate furnishings or buildings.

Dreams of Gems and Precious Metals

Symbols of jewels are common in dreams of wealth, but these precious stones typically appear loose, *not* fashioned into jewelry. Cosmetic jewelry usually represents a *dream of self-understanding*, reflecting vanity or self-consciousness.

Interpreting symbols of jewels or treasure requires understanding of the context in which they occur. These may not be dreams of wealth at all, as with the common theme of *finding treasure guarded by dragons,* which is believed to refer to difficulties encountered in the struggle for knowledge. However, *exceptionally large and glittering jewels* do often represent a desire for material success.

Gold, silver, platinum, and other *precious metals,* especially if they appear in large quantities, represent a desire for material success. However, bright, glittery dream images that feel hollow caution against a *preoccupation* with wealth. Seeking prosperity responsibly is healthy, but this drive needs always to be balanced with a spiritual search and development of natural creative abilities and talents that lie deep within.

Dreams of Money

Money is as powerful a symbol in dreams as it is in waking reality. It symbolizes survival, personal potential, energy, and, for some, self-worth. Not surprisingly, it commonly appears in dreams, more often in the form of coin than currency.

Dreams of money, as all dreams, should be interpreted within the context of the dream's emotions. Money dreams that tend to feel *frantic, insecure, obsessive,* or *shallow* even when the imagery includes vast sums, such as dreaming of finding a treasure chest loaded with money, are particularly revealing. Here are some likely interpretations for these dreams:

+ *Feels frantic:*
  Real financial insecurity or money is too important

+ *Feels worrisome:*
  Wondering where the money is going to come from

+ *Feels obsessive:*
  Money too important; self-worth tied to money

+ *Feels shallow or empty:*
  Money used to compensate for sense of self-worth

The most common dreams of money tend to involve the following symbolism:

- *Finding or hoarding money:*
  Excessive worry about money, real or unwarranted

- *Losing or lack of money:*
  Money is too important, or realistic financial concerns

- *Jealously guarding money:*
  Feeling insecure about financial matters

- *Stolen money:*
  Feeling as if you're being taken advantage of or taken for granted

Typical conscious and unconscious attitudes about money are commonly reflected in the following dream symbolism:

- *Money is too important:*
  Frequent money symbols; frantic over losing money

- *Seeking wealth without responsibility:*
  Careless spending; observing poverty in others without concern
  Huge amounts of wealth but void of satisfaction

- *Realistic concerns about money:*
  Feelings of dread associated with any dream money symbols

- *Obsession or excessive worry about money:*
  Frequent money dreams; finding and hoarding coins

Affirmations for Creating Dreams of Wealth

Dreams of wealth can be powerful tools for creating a reality of prosperity in a responsible manner. Seed your dreams by choosing an affirmation from those that follow, and repeat it to yourself as you fall asleep:

I pass on my prosperity.
I accept that giving and receiving are part of the same circle.
I allow myself to recognize my true ambitions and desires.

I am responsible in my desires.
I am aware of my needs and desires, but not obsessed by them.

My dreams create a reality of prosperity when I honestly recognize what symbols of wealth mean for me and the value I place on money.

Symbols of Work

Work is our most visible symbol of prosperity and is most frequently represented in dreams as *occupations and activities*—from daily chores to career responsibilities.

Most of us spend the majority of our waking hours working—for income, status, identity, and satisfaction. Too often, however, we lack a sense of fulfillment in our job, which leaves us emotionally impoverished. *Symbols of work inform us of our need to seek purpose and value in our everyday efforts.*

Because symbols of work represent deep feelings and attitudes about your profession, expect that they will emerge in dreams when you are questioning the value of your work:

+ Does work bring you a sense of satisfaction?
+ Do you work only for money?
+ Do you feel you're getting the recognition you deserve?
+ Are you seeking more or less responsibility in your job?
+ Do you use work as an escape—are you a workaholic?
+ Are you obsessed by work—is it an emotional need, not a joy?

Dreams of work occur when we're challenged by day-to-day problems on the job. Look at your situation objectively and notice if you are experiencing any of the following symptoms:

- Dreading the beginning of your work week
- Too frequently counting the minutes until a workday is done
- Struggling to maintain enthusiasm about your job
- Getting sick more often than usual

Also ask yourself if your work has changed or deteriorated in any way. For instance:

- Disagreements with superiors or employees
- Any recent specific work-related problems
- Feeling overwhelmed
- Feeling stifled
- Needing to set new interpersonal boundaries in a work situation
- Feeling underutilized or unappreciated

Dreams of work also warn of *imbalance*—focusing excessive energy and attention at the expense of other aspects of life. For workaholics the pendulum has swung too far in one direction, work is no longer balanced by play, and the resulting lack of homeostasis is felt as stress and fatigue. If you feel that your work is an addiction, ask yourself:

- Am I going beyond meeting income needs?
- Am I creating personal fulfillment, or is work an escape?
- Am I balancing my time at work and at play?
- Do I take on too much responsibility?
- Am I relying too heavily on the opinion of others?

Solutions to Work Problems

- *Incubate for clarity:*
  If you have a specific question or dilemma pertaining to work, *incubate* your dreams for guidance. Clarify your goals by asking yourself if you are comfortable with the direction your work is taking. Trust your instincts and realign your

goals if necessary, so that your thoughts and actions are in harmony.

+ *Release your creativity:*
  Remember that you have the abilities to achieve your goals if you're willing to invest the necessary mental and physical energy. Let your creative side guide you a bit more. Create a reality of prosperity by harnessing the creative powers of your dream, tempered by common sense.

+ *Neutralize doubt:*
  The presence of insecurity in a dream suggests that waking doubt, anxiety, and worry are eroding self-confidence. The solution is in *introspection*—use your intuition to bring these doubts into the light, where even the most dark and disconcerting feelings will dissipate.

Animal Symbols of Work

Animal symbols may also represent work and competitive, achievement-oriented drives. Use the following as a guide for interpreting these symbols:

+ *Caged or restricted animals:*
  You may be feeling constrained or restricted. Creativity and expression may be blocked and goals frustrated. *Try giving your impulsive or artistic side a bit more free rein.*

+ *Beasts of burden, such as oxen:*
  These animals symbolize the steady work of life—the necessary but often mundane and sometimes strenuous daily routines.

Look for the *movement* of your dream animal to help interpret its symbolism. If this animal was moving slowly, deliberately, then so are you. Take heart that while you may be slow, your approach is methodical and will eventually get the job done. Don't be discouraged if the results aren't quick and flashy.

Your dream animal may also symbolize *strength of commitment,* a quiet stubbornness—a determination to see some project through to the end.

- *Simians, such as apes or gorillas:*
  These animals, higher on the evolutionary scale, symbolize *creativity and great cunning.* Apes are common dream symbols in nearly all cultures. In China the monkey is believed capable of granting success—but also warns one to guard against mischief makers and monkey business.

  A primate swinging from tree to tree symbolizes *inconsistency*—perhaps your behavior has been a bit erratic lately and your dream is telling you to get a mental grip on yourself.

  A motionless animal is a sign of *conservatism.* If you've been somewhat subdued lately, then it may not be a bad idea to give your creative side a bit more freedom.

  A dream primate that mimics others symbolizes the need to *expand your awareness. Monkey see, monkey do* does little to promote individual achievement, and this symbolism reflects a desire to let your true talents emerge.

CHAPTER FIVE

Dreaming for the Soul

Recently I spent a lunch hour listening to three academics argue the plight of modern society: Why does there seem to be so much individual emotional pain and turmoil? What is the root of global conflict, race hatred, poverty and starvation, malignant nationalism? Are things getting better or are they getting worse?

The three argued various social, political, cultural, economic, even biological reasons for these maladies, but one insight seemed to hold such rich meaning that it stilled all others: *Man has lost his soul.*

Although not a new insight, it is a great truth: *We have lost our soul or, at least, misplaced it.* We have ignored this most important piece of who we are, arguably our very essence, broken off communication with God, and sought to fill our resulting emptiness with everything from power and money to sex and drugs. Since we have done this individually, we have also done so collectively as a society, and we suffer for it. Sadly, we seem to pass on this legacy from generation to generation.

Symptoms of Soullessness

Unfortunately, it is difficult to find something lost if we don't know what to look for. Most agree that we have a soul, but no one really knows what it is, its importance, its meaning. It becomes something much easier to ignore than to wonder about, so our days are consumed with practical matters and we relegate our soul to weekend religion.

But just as we see only the *signs*—the great havoc inside our body—caused by a tiny virus invisible to the naked eye, so do we see only the *symptoms* of soullessness rather than cause of the disease. But these symptoms are apparent and staggering.

+ *Individual symptoms of soullessness:*
    Obsessions and compulsions
    Addiction
    Violence
    Personal void and emptiness
    Emotional stagnation
    Overreliance on intellectualizing and other psychological
        defenses
    Loss of meaning in life
    Suicide

+ *Social symptoms of soullessness:*
    Global conflict and social upheaval
    Bigotry, hatred, and intolerance
    Violence in the name of religious or national fervor
    Poverty and starvation
    Rampant yet preventable disease
    Homicide

Why Do We Have Hunger Pangs of the Soul?

It is part of who we are to yearn for spiritual fulfillment. We can ignore this primal call as many do, or we can misinterpret it as even more do; but like it or not, *spiritual neediness is the essence of being human.*

When we experience feelings of deep emptiness, struggle with disillusionment over the breakdown of our relationships, search insatiably to fix vague yet incessant emotional discomfort, get stuck in revolving-door psychotherapy, find temporary but hollow refuge in addictions, we are being motivated by spiritual need.

Spiritual need is no different from physical or emotional need. For humans to survive, we *must* have certain basics.

• *Physical need:*
   Food, water, air, shelter
   Sex (to survive as a species)

• *Emotional need:*
   Love, security, meaningful human connection

• *Spiritual need:*
   A relationship with God

If we're unable to satisfy any of these fundamental needs, we risk great emotional and physical harm. If physically deprived, we will, of course, die or, as a species, face extinction. When we are emotionally deprived, we suffer loneliness, emotional pain, and in some instances even physical death—infants deprived of love can and do die. Spiritual deprivation is no different and manifests the grave list of individual and societal symptoms just presented.

Many scholars believe that this feeling of a spiritual void is no accident. It is not just a product of modern stress or a mishap of nature, but is instead an intentional and integral part of our humanity. *Our spiritual void is the hunger pang of the soul.* It is built into our creation, put there by God to remind us of our *need* for a spiritual connection, no different from abdominal hunger signaling a need for food.

As a species and as individuals we are incomplete if we lack a relationship with our Higher Power. We were *designed* to be incomplete, we are creatures with a hole made by God, and this essential missing piece can be satisfied only by a spiritual pursuit. Our very purpose for being is to *be with God,* so when we deny this we go against the grain of existence—how can we be comfortable, much less thrive, under these circumstances?

On the other hand, when we cultivate this essential spiritual relationship, we find life rewarding, gain a sense of personal power, are free to develop healthy and lasting human relationships, discover meaning in our daily existence, and secure relief from emotional and physical symptoms.

My dreams create a reality of the soul when I acknowledge
that my spiritual hunger is a call to renew my connection
with my Higher Power.

What Are the Three Levels of the Unconscious Mind?

The unconscious mind is divided into three hierarchical levels,
from top to bottom: *personal, collective, and spiritual.* Most of us are
aware only of the uppermost level, the personal unconscious, but all
are present and available to us through dreams should we desire to
reach them.

The Personal Unconscious

The personal unconscious is what most people consider the unconscious mind to be. This is the reservoir of knowledge and feelings
accumulated over a lifetime that includes our most primitive instincts,
drives, and desires. We cannot, of course, peer directly into the unconscious, and for good reason, as in all likelihood what we would
discover would frighten us beyond belief. Only a small fraction of
these unconscious feelings ever seep into consciousness, as we have
elaborate defense mechanisms that trigger automatically to disguise
this raw material and keep it from overwhelming us.

Nevertheless, the personal unconscious has a profound effect on
determining who we are—our motivations, behavior, feelings, and
attitudes—processing that occurs outside conscious awareness.

We can *glimpse* our personal unconscious mind, and in fact we do
every night, as dreaming is a direct expression to this part of our
psyche.

The Collective Unconscious

The second level of the unconscious mind is what Carl Jung termed
the *collective unconscious.* Jung proposed that hidden deep within
this level of the unconscious mind is the essence of knowledge of all

earlier living beings. It is the same for each of us—this part of the psyche is *shared* and not dependent upon our personal life experiences. Instead it is something we all possess by virtue of membership in the human species.

The contents of the collective unconscious are never consciously known. None of us living today have personally experienced the events that create these realizations, yet our ancestors, human and animal, back to the beginning of life itself contributed this part of our being.

A simple example of the collective unconscious is the almost universal fear of *snakes* that humans possess. Despite the fact that many of us have never experienced a snake firsthand, this creature may still strike fear should we ever be exposed. This fear is derived from the collective unconscious—lessons our distant ancestors have taught us.

Another example of the collective unconscious is the image of *mother.* As infants we immediately recognize and understand mother as the giver of life. We don't need to be taught this knowledge, as it comes to us directly from our collective unconscious.

The collective unconscious provides a kind of *pattern,* a predisposition to act and feel in certain ways. This pattern is by no means fixed and immutable but depends on the experiences each of us as individuals have had in order to determine how this pattern will be expressed. It's much like intelligence: we're all born with a capacity to learn and thereby behave intelligently, but how much we learn and how we act based on this acquired knowledge is determined largely by our life experiences.

The collective unconscious is a reservoir of primordial images called *archetypes.* These are the images from our ancestral past, human and animal, that persist to this day and are shared by people of all races and cultures by virtue of our common lineage. A man in China, a woman in India, a boy in Africa, and a baby in America all share the same archetypal symbols.

Archetypes are old images from the distant past that document our evolution and development as a species. In a sense, buried within each of us are the experiences of our forebears back to the very beginning of human life.

Symbols relevant to early man such as water, fire, mother, or magic, as well as man-made images such as weaponry, are among the archetypal images. These symbols are believed to help us more easily learn and assimilate information vital to our survival. Granted, in today's technological society, instinctively recognizing the image of a spear may seem to have little value. It takes evolution a while to catch up. Most humans stopped using spears only in the last few hundred years—in evolutionary terms just a brief moment in time.

Archetypal images are fascinating and inspire awe. They are a reminder of the interconnectedness of life, the shared heritage of all human beings. It is almost incomprehensible to ponder that buried deep within each of us, even in a limited way, are the experiences of all those who have ever lived.

The Spiritual Unconscious

The deepest level of the unconscious mind is the *spiritual unconscious*. This level transcends the confines of the individual and even the species and connects each of us to the pure energy of the universe. It is a thread that weaves together all life, all matter, all energy, and it is the place where we learn of our purpose, the meaning of our existence.

The spiritual unconscious becomes our focus when we *meditate* or *pray,* and at times we can peer into this part of ourselves through our dreams. This is also where we connect directly with others and the universe around us through *psychic phenomena, dreams of intuition, precognitive dreaming,* and *dream telepathy* (see chapter 6).

The spiritual unconscious is where *deep intuition* originates. Intuition is perceptive insight, *understanding without reasoning,* and it is by far our most underused gift. When we sense a reality, feel it without thinking it, we are using our intuitive powers. Deep intuition appears psychic because it seems to cross time and space; a parent may *feel* his child hurting hundreds of miles away.

Intuition is misunderstood and easily ignored, but it is always present and an expression of the spiritual unconscious. Small children seem more readily able to feel this level of their mind, which explains their uncanny intuitive abilities.

The spiritual unconscious can also be a source of great energy if we allow ourselves access to it. It feels as if we've just meditated— we're invigorated, recharged, and gain strength that comes from deep within. *Dreams of the soul are a direct link to the spiritual unconscious,* which is why they feel alive and empowering.

How Can I Recognize My Dreams of the Soul?

Dreams of the soul are quiet. They whisper yet are persistent with what seems to be the patience of Job. If we ignore them, as we often do, they quietly return, refusing to give up on us. They feel rich, soulful, alive, brimming with meaning even when we don't fully understand their message. If we allow it, they will draw us to them, although they are never demanding.

Dreams of the soul teach us that all relationships require *choice*—no friendship can exist when one forces or imposes oneself on another. Our relationship with God is no different; we must freely choose to make this connection or it is meaningless. But we are also given infinite opportunities to make this choice, and when we seek the Infinite we are never turned away.

Unless we seek them actively, dreams of the soul are rare and most frequently appear following states of physical or emotional shock. Three most common waking realities are associated with these dreams:

1. Profoundly questioning the meaning of life.
Questioning life's meaning is the most common precipitator of dreams of the soul. Many of us, particularly in later years, look back on our lives and begin to wonder, What did I truly accomplish? What is important to me? We try to attach *meaning* to our actions and to justify our history as worthwhile, to gain the sense that somehow we were able to make a dent in the universe.

Less retrospectively, we may ask ourselves if our life's work is what we want. Is there purpose in day-to-day existence? It is during these times that we are more receptive to our Higher Power, and if our search is sincere, we will very likely experience dreams of the soul.

2. Life-threatening experiences.
Traumatically coming face-to-face with one's own mortality often precipitates dreams of the soul. Those who encounter these exceptional human experiences are never left unchanged but are frequently shaken to the core, compelled to reevaluate the meaning in their life.

Near death experiences, terminal illness, the trauma of war, or crime all serve to crystallize our recognition of the reality beyond what we see in everyday life.

3. *Times of painful emotional change.*
Loss of a loved one, illness, divorce, or other painful emotional changes often drive us inward, seeking purpose and searching for the meaning of these shattering events. It forcefully pulls us away from the consuming daily tasks that effectively allow us to avoid a spiritual quest. During these times we usually begin by asking ourselves several questions:

- What is life all about?
- Who am I?
- What is my purpose?
- What is the purpose for this tragedy?
- Why am I here?

Dreams of the soul follow these questions, prompting us to begin to dedicate ourselves to a spiritual quest and yield guidance, direction, and strength.

Recognizing Archetypal Dreams

Archetypal dreams, fragments of the collective unconscious, appear to have an odd feel and quality to them that's difficult to describe but is easily recognizable. They may seem confusing and indistinct, with a slightly *egodystonic* feel, but are rarely disturbing or frightening.

These dreams of the collective unconscious are a product of our genetics and heredity, as our brain inherits the characteristics and experiences of millions of years of evolution, which in a very real sense links us to all humans, prehumans, and animals of our ancestral past. Common archetypal symbols include the following:

- Earth, water, and fire
- Mother, birth, and death
- Magic
- Primitive weaponry
- Reptiles

Pragmatically, dreams of the collective unconscious provide less of a contribution to understanding of our everyday life and personality than do symbols of the personal unconscious, but they are an awesome experience and can sometimes be a gateway to the spiritual unconscious.

Recognizing Dreams of the Spiritual Unconscious

Dreams of the soul touch the spiritual unconscious. They are rare, profound, and moving, yet subtle. They are as distinct from waking reality as can be, and even feel vastly different from dreams of the personal unconscious. They shift focus, their perspective is the eye of the universe and not the individual, so they sometimes challenge our frame of reference.

Dreams of the soul *feel* soulful and quietly alive, usually accompanied by pleasant, soothing imagery, and intuitively seem to carry a rich message. When you feel these dreams, you will likely notice this symbolism:

- Water, usually clear, calm, serene
- Imagery of sacred symbols such as angels or prophets
- Symbols of birth and death, but without fear or darkness
- Symbols of understanding and forgiveness
- Images of childhood
- Beauty, love, attachment
- Faith without doubt

Dreams of the soul teach lessons very different from those of other dreams. They do not solve specific problems or enable creative solutions, they are not insight into personality styles or human relationships, and they do not concern themselves directly with our financial livelihood or other very real everyday worries. But they impact all of these concerns by transcending each of them. Dreams of the soul teach us to *rekindle our spirit and find meaning in daily life* by

- changing priorities.
- searching for personal meaning.

- discovering beauty in our uniqueness.
- clarifying values.
- accepting personal responsibility while transcending self-interest.

My dreams create a reality of the soul when I open myself to my soulful dreams and am receptive to their guidance.

How Can I Cultivate My Spirit Through Dreams?

Just as all dreams do, dreams of the soul *inform* as well as *change* how we feel and act. Fortunately we need simply to experience these dreams, to become aware of them, for their effect to be felt. *And since dreams of the soul create a reality of peace and contentment, it would make sense to encourage them.*

Cultivating dreams of the soul means a willingness to relinquish a tight hold on external reality and accept for the moment a fuzzy second reality that, for most of us, exists only in faith. This may seem impractical or even impossible when financial or other very real concerns of daily living overwhelm us. But acknowledging the spirit doesn't mean escaping to a mountaintop hermitage; it is taking the time to seek meaning in simple everyday activities. This is precisely why dreams of the soul can be so valuable. There's no need to restructure your lifestyle, meditate for hours each day, eat only a specialized diet, or wear sackcloth. Begin simply by attending to your dreams, and since they occur regardless of your intentions, very little effort is involved.

Dreams are a mirror of our waking concerns, so they are most commonly rooted in the personal unconscious, reflecting the day-to-day problems that preoccupy our waking thoughts and feelings. By doing nothing to direct our dreams, they automatically process the issues that consume our energy, what we believe is most important, typically the struggles of the day.

However, we can more actively guide our dreaming. We can focus, if we *consciously* choose, on dreams of the soul, cultivating them by using some combination of *attitude, affirmations,* and *visualizations.*

An Attitude of Soulfulness

The first step in cultivating dreams of the soul is to adopt an attitude of *soulful openness.* This means actively rejecting prejudice and preconception—being *open* to whatever you hear in a dream. *It is preparing yourself to listen and not to judge.* For most of us, this is a considerably more difficult step than it may appear. Almost all of us judge, constantly, automatically, without awareness, as if this habit were built into our being. For instance:

> We judge others *by their appearance when we make a seemingly innocuous remark to ourselves such as "How can they wear that?"*

> We judge ourselves *when we say, "I can't believe I did that."*

> We judge the world *when we find ourselves angered by political activities at home or in some distant country.*

It is probably unrealistic, and perhaps even unwise, to cease all judgment in waking reality, but adopting an attitude of soulfulness means relinquishing the tendency to judge at least our dreams. Doing so increases our receptiveness to spiritual themes, opens our consciousness to new possibilities, deepens our intuition, energizes us, and heightens awareness.

My dreams create a reality of the soul when I adopt an attitude of soulfulness.

Soulful Affirmations

Dreams are responsive; they faithfully reflect our psychological and emotional concerns, so consciously and repeatedly telling ourselves what we want can guide our dreaming. This is the logic of *dream incubation,* our most powerful method of dream guidance. Incubate dreams of the soul by using direct, simple *soulful affirmations* as described in the following three steps.

+ **Step One:**
    Clarify for yourself what it is that you are seeking. Acknowledge where you are psychologically, emotionally, and spiritually at present, and define the direction in which you wish to grow.

+ **Step Two:**
    Choose an affirmation that feels best for you, and repeat it quietly yet deliberately to yourself as you fall asleep, continuing this process for at least a week. Here are some examples of soulful affirmations:

    I am open to the message of my dreams.
    I allow my spiritual unconscious to emerge in my dreams.
    I allow myself a connection with the spirit.
    I seek the guidance of my Higher Self.

+ **Step Three:**
    When you wake in the morning, spend a moment lying still, quiet your mind, and allow any feelings (and they will be subtle) to emerge. You will begin to feel your soulful dreams within just a few days.

Soulful Visualizations

Visualizations are another powerful means of guiding dreams. Visualizations are brief moments of quiet meditation where you construct an image that embodies the spiritual direction you are choosing. A visualization is a kind of imaginal affirmation and operates to increase soulful dreams in the same manner as the incubation process. It is another way of telling yourself what you want and need, focusing your dreaming on these topics.

You do not need an elaborate script or scene to begin a visualization, and it requires only a few moments of quiet time. Follow these three simple steps.

- **Step One:**

  As with verbal affirmations, first clarify for yourself what it is that you are seeking. Ask yourself where you are in the present, what your spiritual needs are, and what you hope to learn.

- **Step Two:**

  Create a simple positive imaginal scene that includes *you,* but the part of you envisioned as your Higher Self. This may be an image of you at peace, loving, nonjudgmental, sincere, confident. The setting you choose is completely up to you; some people prefer serene nature scenes, while others choose to float against a white-lighted background. In this visualization ask yourself what it is that you are seeking, what guidance you hope for, keeping your questions brief and to the point.

- **Step Three:**

  Then, most important, listen quietly for an answer. This response will be immediate, brief, and *felt* as much as *heard.* You may need to resist the temptation to question, even argue with, what you hear. For now just listen; you can think about the content of your message later.

Practicing this visualization method regularly enhances and enriches your dreams of the soul.

My dreams create a reality of the soul when I seek soulful dreams through affirmations and visualizations.

The Six Symbols of the Soul

- Faith
- Innocence
- Inspiration
- Sacredness

- Transformation
- Water

Symbols of Faith

Dreams of faith may contain images of any sort, but themes of *understanding, forgiveness, love, peace,* and *serenity* seem to emerge. Dreams of faith are likely more common than we realize because they, as most dreams of the soul, are subtle and easy to miss.

Faith means belief in the face of uncertainty and does not rest on logical proof or material evidence. Dreams of faith are about believing in yourself and your importance, following your own heart, and feeling charity toward others. They represent finding comfort in an emotional and intellectual belief system that fits you—one that feels right, promotes spiritual values, and encourages you to explore your unique gifts for personal growth. Dreams of faith *feel* peaceful, confident, and secure.

Dreams of faith, as all dreams of the soul, help us to create a reality of contentment. This means finding and resting within an inner peace each moment of every day. For most of us, this seems an impossible goal, but we can fortify ourselves by programming our spiritual dreams for guidance. Incubate your dreams of faith by repeating one of these affirmations quietly to yourself at bedtime:

I think and act deliberately rather than from past fear.
I have the ability to enjoy each moment.
I have no interest in judging myself or others.
I have no interest in conflict.
I am connected with the spirit.
I allow my life to unfold, rather than manipulate.

My dreams create a reality of the soul when I find peace and contentment in faith.

Symbols of Innocence

There is a wonderful story that Dan Millman tells about the inherent spirituality of childhood. A young girl of about four asks her parents to be left alone with her new infant brother. At first her parents are reluctant, wondering why she might make such an odd request. But the child persists, and eventually her parents give in. As the girl enters the baby's room, her parents watch curiously from just outside the door. She approaches her tiny brother, puts her face close to his, and asks quietly, "Baby, tell me what God feels like. I'm starting to forget."

Small children are perfect spiritual beings, still close enough to life before birth that they haven't yet buried the essence of God within them. The concept of *original sin,* that humans are somehow flawed at birth, couldn't be further from the truth and has caused a great deal of social misery. It is the basis for our outdated and overly rigid child-rearing practices, which are designed implicitly to correct this supposed inherent evil but instead perpetuate psychological turmoil and spiritual emptiness. Children are as close to God as we can physically be—it's not what we, as adults, give them that creates healthy growth, it's what we don't take away.

As we grow from baby to child to adult and are faced with the rugged demands of our world, we are frequently diverted from our natural spiritual quest and suffer the discontentment that follows. Symbols of innocence are dreams of the soul that remind us of our spiritual beginning, that we are spiritual beings whose essence and purpose is to establish a relationship with God.

Playful Dreams

Dreams of innocence are sometimes *playful.* They appear when we've forgotten some of the essential ingredients of happiness—innocence, playfulness, and openness—and remind us not to neglect these child-like qualities.

The late philosopher Alan Watts relates a myth where God, in a dream, plays hide-and-seek with Himself. But because there is nothing outside of God, He has no one to play with. He gets over this difficulty by pretending that He is *not* himself—this is His way of hiding from Himself. God pretends that He is all the people of the world, all the plants and animals, all the rocks on earth and stars in the heavens. This way He is able to have wonderful adventures over and over again.

Like God's mythical dream, all of us have the capacity for innocent play when we explore spirituality in our dreams.

The Calming Beauty of Simplicity

Dreams of innocence can remind us of the beauty of simplicity. We clutter our lives with feelings and attitudes that, on close inspection, serve no real purpose and are emotionally draining. Just as we fill our basements, attics, and garages with unneeded and unused stuff, so do we fill our inner selves with unneeded feelings and beliefs.

Innocent simplicity is ridding ourselves of extraneous worry, fear, and judgment.

Dreams of innocence, such as ones that are childlike or playful, are a signal that we have become psychologically overburdened. We've lost contact with our spiritual unconscious and are placing too much importance on things that matter very little. These are common dream symbols of an overextended lifestyle:

+ Clutter, overbearing mess in a dream
+ Feeling overwhelmed
+ Balancing to keep everything from collapsing
+ Feeling or imagery of being boxed in
+ Feelings of helplessness

Lighten your emotional load by recharging your spiritual values, by finding the middle ground between waking and spiritual responsibilities, and by seeking to appreciate simplicity.

A Spiritual Reawakening

While dreams of innocence are somewhat rare, they are spiritually invigorating. They feel wholesome, deep, and sometimes playful and represent the simple innocence of the soul, a youthful reawakening of our natural spiritual potential.

My dreams create a reality of the soul when I allow myself to reawaken the innocent spirituality of my childhood.

Symbols of Inspiration

Inspiration is defined as *divine guidance exerted directly on the mind and soul of humankind.* Dreams of inspiration represent this spiritual guidance, a link to the spiritual unconscious. As with all dreams of the soul, they remind us that we are in essence spiritual beings and that it is important to nurture and care for our soul.

Dreams of inspiration are hopeful, alive, creative. They can themselves be a source of fresh ideas, but they are mostly empowering, leaving us strengthened and energized, freeing our creative spirit. Needless to say, these dreams are a gift, wonderful to experience, and it is not unusual for those around us to notice that we seem lighter, happier, on the mornings that they precede.

Objects of flight are sometimes dreams of inspiration: birds, kites, flying, floating, soaring effortlessly through space. As always, the key to recognizing and understanding dreams of inspiration is how they feel.

Dreams of Birds

Symbols of *birds,* especially colorful ones, are usually dreams of inspiration. In many traditions these creatures are believed to represent a higher state of being, the ability to soar above everyday matters and reach out for something greater than ourselves through hopes and aspirations.

Symbols of colorful birds accompanied by overwhelming feelings of peace and serenity are a particularly wonderful sign, signifying the awakening and soaring of the spirit.

This symbolism sometimes appears when we face a long-standing problem that has eluded resolution and diverted us from our spiritual pursuits. If your dream bird flew freely, then you may finally be rising above what has held you down and regaining your lost vision.

Dreams of Flying

Flying is a common and universal dream symbol. Many of us fly by swimming or otherwise moving through air in a tiring fashion. These common flying dreams are not dreams of inspiration, as inspiration requires no effort.

However, dreams of flight that feel free, effortless, invigorating, and buoyant, as if for the moment nothing could hold you down, that all doubt has vanished, are dreams of inspiration.

Dreams of flying represent a spiritual liberation from self-doubt and uncertainty. These are symbols of spontaneity and unrestrained imagination, just as flight is movement free from gravity.

Dream flight sometimes symbolizes a desire to let our *imagination* soar. They remind us that the limits we set for ourselves are artificial and of our own making and to trust our instincts to guide us. A great height attained in a dream is symbolic of a search for enlightenment and the relinquishing of fear or physical limitations.

Dreams of Floating

Dreams of floating effortlessly through space, if accompanied by peaceful secure feelings, are usually dreams of inspiration. Some New Age thinkers believe that these constitute out-of-body experiences, but they are more likely dreams of the soul.

Dreams of floating also represent a sense of serenity and freedom, symbolized as power over the downward pull of gravity. Movement that is slow and peaceful symbolizes emotional contentment, the ability to rise above self-doubt, and feelings of confidence.

Dreams of Kites and Other Colorful Flying Objects

Kites and other flying objects with a *bright color or sheen* likely represent dreams of inspiration and are a sign of new or renewed spirituality. Interpret these dreams as a reawakening of your spiritual side that will empower you with a greater sense of peace and resolve.

If the flying object ascended beyond your vision, then you may be struggling to gain a clearer picture of your goals or worried that your ambitions seem out of reach. However, these dreams *empower,* giving you the strength and persistence to overcome self-doubt.

Objects that soar but remain in sight suggest clear ambitions as well as the confidence necessary to achieve them. These dreams of inspiration transform disappointment into new hopes and aspirations.

Symbols of Sacredness

Except for water, symbols of sacredness are the most common dreams of the soul and represent the influence of a Higher Spirit on our intuition. They signify the spiritual force and intelligence that guides our lives, providing wisdom and direction if we listen carefully.

Dreams of sacredness usually take on the imagery that we have been taught as children to associate with the divine. At this early age we accepted them with innocent naiveté, even if now as adults we dismiss their importance. And there is, of course, nothing particularly special about the images themselves, but from our childhood conditioning we have come to associate them with the spirit. For those reared in a Judeo-Christian tradition, symbols of sacredness most commonly include the following:

+ Angels
+ Heavenly spirits and powers
+ Jesus and the Apostles
+ Symbols of God, whatever they may be
+ Saints and prophets
+ Heaven
+ Whatever you consider to be divine

Dreams of the soul sometimes reflect a need to clarify spiritual goals by increasing spiritual communication through prayer or meditation. The great psychic Edgar Cayce once described *prayer* as talking to God and *meditation* as listening for the answer. Whichever term we choose to describe our personal reflective time, dreams of sacredness remind us to listen to our intuition and attend to our spiritual needs.

When interpreting dreams of sacredness, ask yourself if you *sensed* a Higher Presence associated with your dream. If you did, listen carefully to your intuition and analyze the symbols contained in this and related dreams. Remember that it's sometimes difficult to sense this presence even when it's there. Preoccupation with daily routines often cloud our receptiveness to dreams, making it difficult to appreciate a transcending spirit. Keep an open mind and look for this presence in your dreams over the next several weeks. It's a sign that your intuition is trying to get a message through.

Feel Your Guiding Intuition

Dreams of sacredness sometimes signify the need for a change in life direction, values, or priorities. They remind us of our special uniqueness, our search for personal meaning, and the importance of or a connection with our Higher Power. They teach us to transcend self-interest and accept greater personal responsibility.

Interpreting these dreams means quieting the noise and clutter of everyday life and fine-tuning your intuition—*feeling* the guidance, the message, of your dream. Use the meditation and visualization strategies described in this chapter to clarify your dream. Finally, don't get discouraged if it doesn't seem to come easily; remember, dreams of the soul are subtle but persistent.

My dreams create a reality of the soul when I feel my guiding intuition.

Symbols of Transformation

These are symbols of great change and metamorphosis and include the seemingly incongruous mix of *birth* and *death*. It may at first seem odd that symbols of death, perhaps life's most painful experience, and symbols of birth, one of our greatest sources of joy, hold similar meaning. But both are *life transitions;* they appear as opposites only because we do not see the ring that binds them together. Birth and death are interwoven facets of a single, never-ending cycle of spirituality.

Symbols of transformation should not, of course, be taken literally —dreaming of death does not foretell that one will die. Rather, these dreams suggest an unconscious change or transition, a readiness to move toward a spiritual understanding. Old beliefs may be withering and dying and a new understanding born. When you experience dreams of transformation, note their *feeling:*

+ Is the change a welcome one?
+ Does this metamorphosis seem growthful?
+ Do you sense an increased awareness accompanying the transformation?
+ Does the change feel right, as if the next step follows naturally?

Dreams of transformation both reflect and foster psychological, emotional, and spiritual growth. They represent a change in attitudes and beliefs as well as a longing to connect with the Universal Consciousness. These dreams also enrich our spirit, and as we grow we become increasingly aware of what's changing us and how spirituality subsumes every other part of our lives.

Dreams of transformation emerge when new attitudes are ripe, new opportunities present themselves, new feelings are acknowledged, and new insights are gained. They are a sign of spiritual empowerment, signaling a move away from preoccupation with material possessions and a return to the essence of life.

Dreams of transformation usually have a positive feeling or tone. Despite the imagery of death, they are hopeful, optimistic, and recognize that life is eternal, continuing on after the body retires. They seem to transcend daily matters to something that feels richer, deeper, encouraging us to keep our spiritual quest alive.

Dreams of Birth

Dreams of birth are powerful symbols of transformation. They represent a new phase of personal growth and development, an awakening of spiritual life; symbolically, from nothing comes being. Psychologically, this process is called *individuation,* the unconscious development and maturation of our psyche.

Dreams of birth include all symbols of new life or the potential for life:

+ Birth and related symbolism
+ Eggs, seeds, and buds

- New blossoms and vegetation
- Springtime

These spiritual images are the seeds of possibility. There is an ancient Greek myth known as the Apple of Hesperides, in which a sweet golden apple is eaten but never diminished. Likewise, dreams of birth represent our abilities and potentials, which are never diminished, even at times when we feel wanting, needy, or insecure.

Dreams of birth may *feel* anxious, painful, or joyous—or some combination, not surprising if you consider that personal and spiritual growth often feels this way.

Dreams of Death

Symbols of birth, the beginning of life, and death, the end of life, while apparent opposites, hold similar meaning. Together they are part of a single unending cycle representing transformation, change, and spiritual growth.

Dreams of death suggest that something is about to end and, therefore, something new and wonderful is about to begin. They are usually a sign that we've become emotionally spent, in need of shrugging off old prejudice that prevents us from realizing growth. For example, many of us raised in a church that we found rigid, outdated, or shallow inadvertently lost our own spirituality when we shunned religion. We may now recognize that we overreacted, that religion is not necessarily synonymous with the spirit, and that it's time to reawaken and nurture our soul.

Use the following as a guide to interpret your dreams of death:

- *Dreams of death that feel hopeful, like a beginning and not an end:*
  Change is imminent, positive, strong; powerful growth

- *Dreams of death that are frightening:*
  Change is feared, being avoided consciously or
    unconsciously

- *Dreams of killing:*
  Change is feared, being avoided with counterproductive
    behaviors

◆ *Dreams of dying:*
 Feeling emotionally and spiritually disconnected and helpless

Dreams of death, as all dreams of transformation, are hopeful, positive, wondrous signs, even when accompanied by frightening imagery. These dreams represent opportunity for growth, understanding, and heightened spiritual awareness.

Symbols of Water

Symbols of water are our most common dreams of the soul and occur in virtually every culture. Water is the source, and therefore the *symbol of life,* not just of mortality, but of eternal spiritual life. Just as water is neither created nor destroyed, but recycled (there is essentially the same amount of water on earth today as there was when our planet was formed), so life and death are merely transitions in the state of awareness.

Water is an archetypal symbol with only subtle differences in meaning across cultures, much like the many dialects of a single language. All mythologies regard the image of water as a powerful symbol:

- ◆ In Indian mythology, the world floats in healing waters.
- ◆ In Islam and Hinduism, water purifies and cleanses.
- ◆ In psychoanalysis, water represents the power of the unconscious.
- ◆ Christianity uses water for baptism, awakening the spirit.
- ◆ New Age experts see water as a symbol of the universal healer.
- ◆ Native American traditions believe water to be life giving.

Symbols of water may vary in dreams by clarity, temperature, or motion. Use the following as an interpretive guide:

+ *Clear, sparkling water:*
    Clarity of spiritual feeling
    Confidence, hope, and a sense of personal power
    Health and long life

+ *Dark, muddy water:*
    Indecision, worry, and a loss of spiritual connection
    Overly influenced by secular circumstances and concerns

+ *Calm, soothing water:*
    Rekindling the spirit, baptism
    Spiritual peace, serenity

+ *Turbulent, raging water:*
    Spiritual war, struggling with a desire to balance spiritual
        and secular concerns

+ *Contained or stagnant water:*
    Conformity, pressure to act on the will of a group
    Overly concerned with secular matters

+ *Frozen water:*
    Refusing to acknowledge the spirit

Dreams of water may appear during those times when we come face-to-face with the symptoms of soullessness: a stifling, choking loss of meaning, love, and purpose. Therefore these dreams sometimes emerge when we

+ neglect our unique talents and gifts.
+ ignore our responsibility to use our talents to
  help others.
+ refuse to love ourselves, God, and others.
+ are too concerned with material possessions.
+ shun insight and spiritual wisdom.
+ question our values and spiritual needs.

Water is a symbol of rebirth. It reminds us of the ceaseless opportunities we are given to reestablish a relationship with our Higher Power. These dreams continue over a lifetime, quietly, patiently calling us back to our spiritual beginnings, the true purpose for our existence.

My dreams create a reality of the soul when I accept them as a gentle yet persistent nudge to reestablish a personal relationship with my Higher Power.

CHAPTER SIX

Dreaming for Prophecy

⁓ Dreams of prophecy are rare and wonderful. They are the most controversial and misunderstood of all dreams largely because we misunderstand our own intuitive abilities. Prophecy literally means *a divinely inspired prediction of the future;* however, these dreams might better be termed *dreams of intuition* because the psychic connotation of this definition is misleading.

When we dream of prophecy we do sense possible future events, but usually not in a manner considered *psychic* and certainly not because the future is predetermined. Instead we *feel* these events in our dreams; we become so attuned to information stored in our unconscious mind, to the subtle influences of waking consciousness on dream reality, and to the energy of the universe that we begin to *sense* how certain circumstances may unfold.

By far, most dreams of prophecy are not mysterious or even psychic in the traditional sense. But they are a testament to the vast power of the unconscious mind, personal, collective, and spiritual, and perhaps more than any other form of dreaming, they can deepen and enrich our human experience.

Dreams of prophecy fall into two categories: those that reflect heightened *intuition* and so-called *paranormal* dreams.

What Are My Dreams of Intuition?

If we allow, intuition can be a powerful guiding force in our lives. There is nothing unscientific or even mysterious about our intuitive abilities. They are not the exclusive province of a gifted few, as all of us possess natural intuitive skills, although we accept and use our talents in varying degrees.

Intuition is *immediate knowing or sensing, seemingly without logic and reason.* It is perceptive insight, trusting impressions when cause is not evident to our physical senses. Because intuition appears to bypass rationality, we are suspicious and often reluctant to accept this rich source of information. But intuition *is* logical, just not what we consider waking logic, as it taps the resources of the personal, collective, and spiritual unconscious mind.

Intuition and Personal Unconscious

The personal unconscious is amazingly receptive and sensitive, constantly gathering a multitude of environmental cues that elude conscious awareness. For instance, subtle changes in another's behavior, such as choice of words, tone of voice, or body language, may be ignored consciously but are actively processed by the personal unconscious.

These data are stored, never lost, yet rarely accessed. However, if we were able to make use of this information, we would be in a position to make better predictions and enhance our understanding of many situations simply because we have more and better data on which to base our decisions. Fortunately this subtle information is always available to us through the personal unconscious. Tapping this unseen material is called *using our intuition.*

Dreams of intuition are saturated with the knowledge of our personal unconscious. What we missed while awake reveals itself in our sleep. We remember, for instance, that we felt slightly unsettled by the *way* our boss told us a bit of news, yet since nothing was overt, we managed to ignore these feelings—only to have them surface again in a dream.

Fortunately, when we recall dreams of intuition, they usually make sense, in that the information initially lost to consciousness is put into proper context. These dreams may vary greatly in their symbolism, and while some are overpowering, most feel muted yet persistent. Here are some characteristics of dream symbolism representative of the personal unconscious:

+ Unusually detailed, as if calling your attention to something
+ Subtle yet persistent feeling that a dream contains a message
+ Unsettling or restless feeling in a dream
+ Dreams whose memory lingers tenaciously after you wake

The Deep Intuition of Our Spiritual Unconscious

When we perceive a reality by feeling it without thinking it, and possess an understanding of events that rationally seems impossible for us to know, it's likely we're attuned to the deep intuition of our spiritual unconscious. This part of our mind is most receptive to psychic energy and therefore is unrestrained by time and space. At times we can *sense* that a loved one is pained or in danger, even hundreds of miles away:

> I dreamed that my brother, whom I hadn't seen in some time, was in terrible danger. He was hiking and stopped to rest when suddenly a huge boulder, the size of a house, began to tumble down the mountainside, threatening to crush him. I was amazed, because the giant rock made such a deafening noise and vibration as it crashed down the cliff, yet my brother just sat there, oblivious of the danger. . . .

Needless to say, the dreamer found her dream distressing, with images and impressions that nagged for days until she was finally able to clarify the dream's circumstances by tracking down the whereabouts of her brother.

On the night of this dream, the boy had been driving on a narrow mountain road when suddenly a drunk driver, screeching around the bend, crashed into the boy's car, sending him over a small embankment. The dreamer tracked her brother to a local rural hospital, where the boy was recovering from his injuries.

Many dreams of intuition, as this one, trouble the mind for days even when we attempt consciously to ignore their feeling.

Dreams of deep intuition are rare and usually occur under personally stressful or extreme circumstances. But they are also wonderful in that they tie us together with others who are important in our lives, evidence that none of us are truly alone but all a part of a larger whole.

Synchronicity

Intuition is learning to recognize the natural interconnectedness of all life. These connections can be evident in waking reality if we observe closely, and they certainly appear in our dreams of prophecy.

Random life events are rare, if they exist at all, but causal meaning is often hidden from waking logic. That's because the *cause* of many life circumstances cannot be found in the physical causality that we have become accustomed to accepting. Force, velocity, gravity, and movement are examples of physical cause and effect commonly observed and understood through waking reality. But these phenomena represent only a small portion of universal energy. The remaining *psychic* energy, obscured by our preoccupation with physical reality, is as real and influential, but is easily ignored.

Like the flow of physical energy, psychic energy moves automatically, without conscious awareness, and is responsible for the meaningful coincidences that fill our lives. Jung called these coincidences *synchronicity*. They are the unseen causal link gluing together life events that might otherwise appear random.

Synchronistic connections are never obvious in the physical world because the causal link is formed at a much deeper level than is observable through waking reality. They are evidence of the *oneness* of the universe, connecting each of us through the spiritual unconscious.

Synchronistic events seem to occur when we need them the most. This is not surprising, as the universe is highly responsive to our needs. When we do for ourselves as best we are able, but in good faith still fall short, somehow what we need appears—people, money, or emotional support all seem to enter our life just at the right moment. And if we're listening, dreams of prophecy also emerge powerfully during these times of need.

Synchronicity is recognizable in our dreams of prophecy. However, finding meaningful coincidences in dreams requires some practice and, like most of reality, is a dual process of observation and active creation. Dream synchronicity can be facilitated by

- consciously acknowledging the interconnectedness of all life events.
- expecting to find this meaning in your dreams of prophecy.
- attending to any unsettling feelings or restless energy in dream.
- attending to dreams whose memory seems to linger well into daytime.
- trusting your intuition.
- tracking dreams of intuition in your dream journal.

My dreams create a reality of prophecy when I search for the meaning of coincidence in everyday life.

Blocked Intuition

Dreams of prophecy alert us when we are consciously or unconsciously *blocking* our intuitive powers. It may seem odd that this should occur, but it is actually quite common. If we sense something that we don't want to know, it is often less psychologically threatening to ignore our intuition than it is to accept it. We block these feelings and operate under a false, deceptively safe illusion. Of course, this strategy never works in the long run, as the reality of the situation will eventually force us to face what we have denied.

Dreams of prophecy warn us that we are on an emotionally dangerous course by ignoring this psychologically valuable information. In such circumstances, the following dream symbolism tends to emerge:

- Dreaming of self as unpopular or unheard
- Excessive ridicule, rejection, or criticism in a dream
- Feeling a distinct lack of support or alone
- Frustrating misunderstandings in dreams
- A sense of dread; something unpleasant is imminent

My dreams create a reality of prophecy when I trust and value my intuition.

What Are Paranormal Dreams?

Precognitive and telepathic dreams are called *paranormal,* or *psi.* They are similar to what we consider clairvoyance and telepathy except that they occur while we are dreaming. *Precognitive* dreams are clairvoyant, accurately predicting unlikely future events, while *telepathic* dreaming refers to remote dream communication between two or more individuals.

These are the most controversial of all dreams of prophecy, and while most dream experts acknowledge their existence, they are by no means universally accepted. However, precognitive and telepathic dreams have been reported anecdotally in nearly all cultures.

Dreams of the Future

Precognitive dreams, those that correctly represent unlikely future events, are rare and sometimes dramatic. Most dream books recount a list of anecdotal stories of precognition, but in reality dreaming of the future, at least in a strictly psychic way, is unusual. For instance, in the *Registry for Prophetic Dreams,* only forty-eight of eight thousand precognitive dreams were verified as authentic. Clairvoyant dreams do exist, but not in great frequency.

In *Our Dreaming Mind,* Dr. Robert Van de Castle cites Mark

Twain's (Samuel Clemens's) unsettling dream predicting his brother's death—a classic example of precognition:

> Clemens dreamed of a metal coffin containing the body of his brother, Henry, adorned with a large bouquet of white flowers surrounding a single crimson rose.

A few days following his dream, Clemens learned of an explosion aboard a Mississippi riverboat that killed many of the passengers and crew, including his brother. When Clemens arrived at the morgue, he found Henry's body lying in a metal coffin with a bouquet of white and crimson flowers resting on his chest.

Dreams such as this one, dramatic and unexplainable, catch our attention so are frequently mentioned in dream books, giving the impression that they occur with greater frequency than they actually do.

Precognitive dreams tend to foretell dramatic, painful, or grisly events. They often precede natural disasters, crime, life-endangering accidents, or catastrophic illness and are rarely associated with joyful or pleasant circumstances. Following are the most prominent themes of precognitive dreams:

- Death, 50 percent
- Accidents, 30 percent
- Injury, 10 percent
- Other (illness and personal catastrophic events), 10 percent

They seem somewhat fatalistic, premonitions that one has little opportunity for altering. Because of this, their purpose is unclear, as to simply predict a catastrophic future with no hope of change seems, on the face of it, pointless. However, if we do not understand the larger context in which these dreams occur, it is difficult to make judgments of their value.

Big Dreams

On rare occasions, some precognitive dreams seem to be shared by many dreamers. These dreams are associated with conflict of such unique intensity that it places great stress on society's ability to cope or adapt. Plague, natural disasters, global war, or other cataclysmic world events may give rise to these special dreams.

Jung called these extremely powerful shared dream experiences *big dreams* and cites the example of many Germans who, in the 1930s, dreamed of a *blond beast,* a reference to the horrors of Hitler's Nazis.

Big dreams sometimes emerge in archetypal form. They tap ancient symbolism shared by all humans through the collective unconscious and seem remote from one's personal life. Their images appear strange and uncanny, difficult to discern, but they have a powerfully distinctive feel.

Fortunately, most of us will never experience a *big dream,* as these unique dream experiences are associated with life-shattering social catastrophes.

Characteristics of Precognitive Dreams

Precognitive dreams are often described as unmistakable, unusual, very different from a dreamer's typical experience. They stand out, are not easily forgotten, and may linger in an unsettling manner after the dreamer wakes. In our culture women are twice as likely as men to experience these dreams. They most frequently symbolize men, typically a spouse, family member, or friend. Precognitive dreams commonly possess the following characteristics:

+ Rare and unpredictable
+ Extremely vivid and intense
+ Unmistakable, difficult to forget
+ Memory lingers tenaciously after the dreamer wakes
+ More complete than typical dreams
+ Less obscured by personal symbolism
+ Feels unsettling

Dream Telepathy

Dream telepathy refers to remote dream communication between two or more individuals. It is analogous to waking telepathy, where one attempts to transmit a psychic message to someone else. In dreams this phenomenon is said to have occurred when one person telepathically influences another's dreams.

Dream telepathy is the most controversial form of paranormal dreaming as well as the most uncommon—telepathic dreams are not frequently reported outside of experimental sleep and dream laboratories.

The Maimonides Project

The most systematic experimental study of dream telepathy was the 1962 Maimonides Project, named for the New York hospital where it was conducted. While several studies were included in the Maimonides research, the basic paradigm was as follows:

An individual sleeping in the dream laboratory (called the *receiver*) was monitored as to when they entered REM, a signal that dreaming had likely begun. At that time a *sender* in a separate room would mentally concentrate on some predetermined image, attempting telepathically to send it into the sleeper's dream. The following morning the sleeper was shown a series of pictures and asked to rank them as to the likelihood that they were the actual image sent during the night.

Thirteen separate studies were conducted at Maimonides, with nine of these obtaining statistically significant results. These overall results suggest the reality of dream telepathy, but as with all scientific research, conclusions regarding the Maimonides Project are open to great debate. Psychic phenomena, in general, have been notoriously difficult to prove scientifically, and paranormal dreams are no exception.

The personal significance of telepathic dreams is also open to question. Since these dreams are so rarely found outside of laboratory conditions, it is not known what purpose they serve. As with other paranormal dreams, telepathy remains an intriguing mystery.

How Can I Create Dreams of Prophecy?

Dreams of intuition appear most responsive to conscious efforts to increase their frequency. We can noticeably increase the number and depth of our intuitive dreams by using the methods described in the pages that follow. However, it is questionable whether we are able to create paranormal dreams, such as precognitive experiences. These rare dreams seem to occur spontaneously and unpredictably, and techniques to increase their frequency are not usually met with success.

Creating dreams of intuition requires patience and practice but is well worth the effort. This is a more advanced exercise, as it taps lower levels of the unconscious mind, the collective and spiritual unconscious.

Adopting an Attitude of Deep Awareness

It's important to adopt an attitude consistent with the message and spirit of these dreams. Recognize that dreams of prophecy are rarely dramatic, despite what popular dream books and magazines may imply. Instead, your most powerful dream messages are wonderfully simple and reflect intuition about activities of everyday life. Adopting an attitude of intuition means

+ accepting that dreams of prophecy are not dramatic but represent daily life.
+ placing value on subtleties.
+ seeking intuition for self-growth and understanding not vanity.
+ exercising patience.
+ maintaining confidence and an expectation of success.

Heightening Waking Intuition

One of the best ways to increase dreams of prophecy is learning to heighten *waking* intuition. Remember that dreams are responsive; they will focus on whatever emotional, psychological, or physical state is important to us at the time. When we are preoccupied with financial concerns, for example, we experience a greater frequency of prosperity dreams. So to increase your dreams of intuition, send a message to your subconscious that you wish to enhance your intuitive abilities, and you'll find that this priority will automatically be reflected in your dreams.

Heightening waking intuition means, among other things, becoming *more aware* of your environment. Follow these three steps:

- *Step One: Notice the details of your environment.*
  Consciously slow down, take deeper breaths, even to the extent that you become aware of your breathing. Spend the time and energy to notice the fine details of the scenery around you. Engage *all* of your senses, not just sight and hearing, but also smell, taste, and touch. Mentally note what you have been missing until you are able to view your environment from a completely new perspective.

- *Step Two: Sensing others' energy.*
  When you are with other people and have the opportunity, closely study each individual around you. Listen carefully to what they are saying, notice their tone of voice, the way they move, and their dress, body language, unique mannerisms, and energy level. Get a sense of their level of self-confidence, their openness and sincerity. Make a mental list of how you would describe them, focusing on the subtleties, characteristics that you notice now but have previously overlooked.

- *Step Three: Feeling your emotional reactions.*
  Finally, pay attention to how *you* feel while interacting with someone. Honest feelings are guided by intuition and are a great source of information. Note if the interaction felt

  - calming
  - content and comfortable
  - open and honest
  - nervous or angry
  - sad or needy
  - superficial

The emotions you experience in waking intuition are much the same as those you feel in your dreams of prophecy, so becoming attuned to these feelings is beneficial for understanding both realities. Expect that soon after you begin exercising these intuitive skills, your dreams of prophecy will begin to emerge with greater frequency.

Incubating Dreams of Prophecy

Dream incubation is the single most powerful method for creating dreams of prophecy. The incubation process is the same for these dreams as it is for any and involves the following three steps:

♦ *Step One:*

Clarify what it is that you are seeking. For dreams of prophecy, this usually means finding, sharpening, and interpreting intuition. Ask yourself why you are searching, what you hope to learn, and how this knowledge will benefit you and those around you.

♦ *Step Two:*

Choose an affirmation that *feels* best for you and repeat it quietly yet deliberately to yourself as you fall asleep. Be sure to continue this process for at least a week. Here are some examples of prophecy affirmations:

I appreciate my intuitive abilities.
I am open to the guidance of my spiritual unconscious.
I trust my intuition.
I allow myself to retain the message of my dreams.
I allow my spiritual unconscious to emerge in my dreams.

♦ *Step Three:*

When you wake in the morning, spend a moment lying still, quiet your mind, and allow any feelings to emerge. Pay particular attention to those dreams that offer subtle guidance—for instance, the meaning of an overlooked behavior during some waking interaction.

Recognize that *dramatic* dreams of prophecy are rare, so do not become discouraged. When you experience *any* dream of prophecy, acknowledge it, trust it, and note it in your dream journal.

My dreams create a reality of prophecy when I acknowledge and trust my dreams of prophecy.

The Three Symbols of Prophecy

+ Clairvoyance
+ Intuition
+ Magic

Symbols of Clairvoyance

Clairvoyance refers to the *power to see or foretell events that cannot ordinarily be perceived by the senses*. Dreams of clairvoyance are analogous to waking *extrasensory perception*—psychic dream states inexplicably informing one of remote events, foretelling the future, or telepathically communicating with someone.

Unfortunately, little scientific evidence is available to document these dreams. As with all psychic phenomena, dreams of clairvoyance are not well understood and are therefore controversial. However, it's naive to believe that current science can explain all human mysteries, and the reality of these dreams cannot be dismissed simply because we are unable to reproduce them in a laboratory.

Dreams of clairvoyance are reported in nearly all cultures, each with its own system for interpreting and explaining the prophecy. The biblical definition of a *prophet* is someone who *never* makes an incorrect prediction. It was believed that one mistaken omen and the prophet's abilities could no longer be attributed to divine intervention. By this definition there are few, if any, modern-day prophets, as no psychic is infallible. Likewise, no one's dreams could be considered truly prophetic because they err too frequently. However, this standard may be unduly restrictive, as even one remarkable premonition in one hundred can be stunning.

We do know that dreams of clairvoyance appear to be very rare, tend to be experienced more by women than by men, and usually foretell ominous rather than pleasant events.

But if you feel that your dream contained a *premonition*, keep an open mind, seek to verify the experience, and note your dream symbols over the next several nights. It would seem likely that your premonition will reemerge in some form if it truly exists.

Recognizing Dreams of Clairvoyance

Dreams of clairvoyance possess an *unmistakable tone,* difficult to describe but obvious to those who experience them. They do not seem to share any specific or common imagery, although they are usually vivid and intense and *feel* as if they are communicating a message.

These dreams stand out; they are very different from a dreamer's typical experience, and their memory sometimes lingers for days in an unsettling way. Dreams of clairvoyance often possess the following characteristics:

+ Rare and unpredictable
+ Extremely vivid and intense
+ Unmistakable, difficult to forget
+ Memory lingers tenaciously after the dreamer wakes
+ Short but more complete than other dreams
+ Less obscured by personal symbolism
+ Feels unsettling

Spiritual and Psychological Meaning of Prophetic Dreams

Dreams of clairvoyance may be interpreted from a spiritual perspective. If you *feel* a premonition in your dream, it's possible that you're attuned to your spiritual unconscious and are under the guidance of a Higher Being. Your dream may contain a prophetic message or it may be a sign to follow the direction of your intuition in a spiritual matter, perhaps symbolizing hidden power, creativity, and unseen potential within yourself that's been neglected.

Psychologically, dreams of clairvoyance may represent a striving for knowledge, being receptive to new ideas and impressions. If there was a *transparent quality* to any dream image, it may represent a sudden realization, a matter becoming crystal clear.

Symbols of Intuition

Dreams of intuition are the most common manifestations of dream prophecy and perhaps the most important. They may also be the most misunderstood, as these dreams are usually subtle and not the dramatic premonitions that many of us have come to believe ought to constitute prophetic abilities.

Because these dreams are quiet, and because they often don't match our expectations, we miss them, mistakenly ignore them, and misinterpret them. It's likely, then, that their frequency is far greater than we realize and their meaning deeper than we immediately comprehend.

Dreams of intuition possess *acute intuitive insight and perceptiveness*. They appear illogical to a rational mind because they bypass the physical senses and tap the resources of the personal, collective, and spiritual unconscious. However, there is nothing unscientific or even mysterious about these intuitive dreams. They are as natural as any form of communication, just one we haven't yet learned to trust.

When we hear of others who experience these dreams, we are tempted to believe that the dreamer has some special intuitive powers most people don't possess. But dreams of intuition are not the exclusive province of a gifted few; we all innately possess these abilities, although we may be reluctant to trust and apply what we learn.

Dreams of intuition often originate in the deepest level of the unconscious mind, the *spiritual unconscious*. This is the part of our mind that transcends the confines of the individual and even the species and connects each of us to the pure energy of the universe. It is a thread that weaves together all life, all matter, all energy, and therefore allows us access to information unbounded by time and space. When we *feel* a loved one's pain hundreds of miles away, it is an expression of our connected spiritual unconscious.

Interpreting Dreams of Intuition

Dreams of intuition are apparent by their *feel*. They vary greatly in imagery, and while some are overpowering, most feel muted and can be easily ignored. However, they are uniformly *persistent* and will recur over time, and they are *reassuring* even when they alert us to danger.

Dreams of intuition usually involve people we know personally. In fact, if a dream premonition refers to a stranger, particularly a famous one such as the president or pope, then it is very likely a dream of clairvoyance and not intuition.

Here are some further characteristics of dreams of intuition:

+ A dream that feels alive but not agitated
+ A persistent message but without urgency
+ Reflective, not impulsive
+ Lovingly reassuring and encouraging regardless of the message
+ Suggestive of simplicity of action, not major life changes
+ Never based on fear or unhealthy guilt
+ Does not contradict common sense

Dreams of intuition are powerful teachers, but, like all dreams, their guidance should be balanced by common sense and rationality.

Symbols of Magic

Dreams of magic can reach deep into the collective unconscious, tapping powerful archetypal symbolism such as alchemy or sorcery.

The collective unconscious is a reservoir of archetypes (primordial images). These are the essence of experience of all earlier living beings, human and prehuman, back to the beginning of life itself. Archetypal images do not depend upon personal experience but are shared by people of all races and cultures, something we possess by the simple virtue of membership in the human species.

Dreams of magic sometimes tap this symbolism and represent the contents of the collective unconscious.

Archetypal Dreams of Magic

Dreams of magic are somewhat rare and tend to include the following symbolism:

• alchemy	• magic	• sorcery
• animism	• mysticism	• voodoo
• goddess	• occult	• witchcraft
• haunting	• shamanism	• wizardry

Dreams of magic that represent archetypal images often have an odd feel or quality to them that's difficult to describe but is easily recognized. They may seem confusing or appear indistinct. They feel slightly *egodystonic*—as if they're coming from somewhere else, that they are not just your own. However, these dreams are rarely disturbing or frightening.

Alchemy

Dreams of magic sometimes just precede or follow life changes. This is probably related to the archetypal importance of *alchemy*, a powerful symbol of transition. Alchemy literally refers to medieval chemical attempts to transmute base metals into gold, discover the panacea, and prepare an elixir of longevity.

However, alchemy is also an archetypal symbol representing a deep yearning for immortality and omnipotence—since we are like God, it is our desire to be God. The magical process of transmuting worthless metal into gold symbolizes the power of creation.

Dreams of alchemy may refer to psychological and emotional growth. These symbols accompany life transitions and represent a yearning for the spiritual guidance that gives meaning to these changes.

APPENDIX ONE

How to Remember Your Dreams

Dream research has consistently shown that human beings have at least five to six dreams every night. Yet for many, dreams remain extraordinarily elusive—some don't remember their dreams at all; others recall them only on occasion; and still others claim they simply never dream. But it's impossible *not* to dream, and fortunately it's easy to learn how to remember dreams. This appendix will teach you how to successfully remember and journal your dreams.

Rapid Eye Movement

Dreaming is done primarily, but not exclusively, in a stage of sleep known as *REM*, or *rapid eye movement*. It's called this because a sleeper in this stage will characteristically display quick, jerky eye movements that can be readily observed below their closed eyelids.

On average, we first enter REM about an hour after falling asleep, although this dream period lasts only about ten minutes. Then, about every ninety minutes or so, we enter REM again. This makes about five to six REM periods for an average night's sleep. The length of each REM period, and therefore the amount of time we spend dreaming, increases slightly over the course of the night. The last REM period, our most productive dream time, is also the longest, lasting about thirty minutes and occurring just prior to waking in the morning.

With a hand calculator you can figure that the average person spends more than five years in REM sleep and therefore in dreams.

Why Can't I
Remember My Dreams?

Despite all this dreaming, it's not unusual to experience difficulty remembering our dreams. As you might expect, several theories attempt to explain why we fail to recall dreams. Researchers have looked at personality, creativity, intelligence, motivation, ratings of dream importance, sleep schedules and environment, and many other factors.

Freud believed that people forget (repress) their dreams because they represent emotional material too traumatic to be remembered. In his view dreams represent an ongoing psychic conflict that's hidden in the subconscious. This repressed material occasionally filters into consciousness via dreams but is then immediately *forgotten* when the dreamer wakes.

Most psychologists today believe that while this sort of repression does occur, it is not a significant reason for forgetting dreams. Many traumatic memories are indeed suppressed if they reach consciousness before the individual is ready to assimilate them into conscious awareness, but this process occurs when we're awake as well as when we're asleep, and dreams are usually sufficiently disguised to protect us from being overwhelmed.

But it's far easier, or what scientists would call more *parsimonious,* to explain difficulty in recalling dreams using simpler explanations. Rest assured that, despite Freud, if you're having trouble remembering your dreams, it doesn't mean you have psychological or emotional problems.

There is no single reason that will explain every lost dream. Here are some of the most common problems that I have encountered in teaching people to remember their dreams:

◆ *I don't believe dreams are important.*

It would seem obvious that if you don't believe in what you're doing, no matter what it is, you won't do it well. If dreams are of little value to you, why remember them? Unfortunately this is a common sentiment in our culture, where dreaming is considered little more than an amusing anomaly, certainly not a particularly worthwhile experience that should be carefully observed. But in cultures where dreaming is highly prized, virtually everyone remembers their dreams.

The reality of dreams is not questioned in many primitive cultures. If a *Kamchatka* native dreams that a possession of his was given away, no matter how valuable, he does give it away when he wakes.

The *Zulu* regard dreams of suffocation with horror. Such dreams are believed to predict death and may even precipitate an anxiety attack so severe as to require hospitalization. And if a Zulu man dreams that a friend tries to kill him, he immediately severs his relationship with this person.

Nearly all Native American tribes place great significance in dreams. The *Crow* learn of new medical remedies and bountiful hunting grounds through dreaming. Young *Huron* Indians learn about the invisible world by dreams produced through fasting. *Hopi* Indians believe dreams to be visions—prophetic and guides to living.

The *Ojibwa of Manitoba* consider dreams to be an *actual* experience of the self, no different from a waking adventure. Likewise, the *Zuni of New Mexico* consider the experience of dreaming *actually doing something*—not simply a description of behaviors.

Probably the most striking example of a belief in the importance and reality of dreams comes from the natives of *Gabon*. This culture uses dreams as a kind of legal evidence. Dreams are believed to be messages from the dead, who are constantly watching over the tribe. Since these dead tribal members have the distinct benefit of omnipotence, they guide the living in making judgments and decisions through dream communication.

+ *I've never tried to remember my dreams.*

Remembering dreams is actually a skill, and like any skill, it requires some practice to master. If you've *never* intentionally tried to recall a night's dreams, chances are you haven't mastered the skills to do so. Fortunately this is an easy skill to learn—one of the easiest things you'll ever do—but it does take a bit of practice. And as with most things, just doing it makes you better at it. In the following pages I'll discuss some simple ways to get started.

+ *I'm just too busy to remember my dreams.*

People often forget their dreams when they're too busy or rushed in waking life. Dream recall is facilitated by a calm, peaceful attitude and hampered when one is so stressed that attending to dreaming loses its priority.

It's best to adopt a passive attitude, one that allows you to remember, not one that forcefully demands your attention.

• I'm just too tired to remember my dreams.

The amount of sleep you get is another factor affecting dream recall. Insufficient sleep increases stress, irritability, and loss of focus on dreaming, not to mention other problems. If you're always tired, it's much more difficult to recall and enjoy your dreams, much less anything else in life. Regular sleep patterns also help, by conditioning dream recall as a habit.

• I remembered a dream this morning, but now I forgot.

Even the most skillful dreamer will forget the night's adventures over the course of a busy day. Dreams don't compete well for memory with everything going on in our waking lives. It's always best to record your dreams first thing on awakening.

Many dreamers keep a small notebook and pen by their bedside to record their dreams first thing in the morning, but if this isn't realistic, record your dreams *whenever* you remember them. Enter them into your *DreamScape* journal whenever you have the opportunity.

What Are Some Simple Strategies for Remembering My Dreams?

If you've never really remembered your dreams in the past and would like to now, it's best to start your journey at a time when you're getting enough sleep and not under particularly severe or chronic stress. If your life is extremely chaotic right now, cope with the source of this stress before beginning any new projects, including dreamwork.

The key to remembering dreams is *habit*. Think of dream recall as a skill—and like any new skill, it takes repetition and practice. You are conditioning yourself to do something new, but once the conditioning is established, dream recall becomes second nature and you'll find yourself remembering a rich variety of dream experiences every night.

Here are some simple and interesting strategies you might try to help yourself remember your dreams:

The Affirmation Technique

Fortunately, the easiest dream recall method is also one of the most effective. It's called the *affirmation technique*, a kind of self-hypnosis.

Affirmations are brief, positive, deliberate statements that you say quietly to yourself in order to program your subconscious to provide a desired outcome. The technique goes like this:

At bedtime quietly repeat a simple affirmation to yourself, like the ones that follow, as you fall asleep. You may notice yourself entering an altered state of consciousness just prior to dozing off, one in which images seem odd, sometimes more intense. This is called the *hypnagogic state*—you're half-asleep but still aware enough to consciously perform an affirmation.

Many dream experts believe that we're very receptive to suggestion in this state, and since affirmations are a form of self-hypnosis, they're powerful and likely to be followed by your subconscious mind. In fact, advanced dreamers use affirmations to program their dreams to create certain outcomes, such as health remedies or spiritual guidance. This is called the *incubation method,* and it is a powerful tool for creating dream reality.

Affirmations are highly personal, and there's no right or wrong way of using this technique. The idea is to condition yourself to be more receptive to remembering your dreams and to create a positive expectation.

It's best to keep each affirmation short, direct, positive, self-affirming. Avoid being demanding or critical—don't force it. And don't judge your progress; just allow the process to happen.

Dream recall is a natural process and will occur on its own if you simply allow it to.

Try one of these affirmations, or make up one of your own:

I am freely able to remember my dreams.

I allow my subconscious to speak to me through my dreams.

I am becoming more and more aware of my dreams.

I am open and receptive to my dreams.

*I allow myself to experience and recall my dream feelings with great
   clarity.*

Remembering my dreams is natural and effortless.

Most novice dreamers report some dream recall within a week of beginning the affirmation technique. But if it takes you a little longer, take heart. We're all unique, and not every method works the same for everyone.

The Self-Hypnosis Method

In *Creative Dream Analysis,* dream expert Dr. Gary Yamamoto describes a more direct form of self-hypnosis than the affirmation method. It relies on *direct suggestion* accompanied by a symbolic act that presumably reinforces the suggestion and prompts memory. Here's how it works:

Put a glass of water by your bed. At bedtime drink half of the glass while you make an affirmation, such as "Drinking half of this glass of water will prepare me to remember my dreams. When I awake, I'll drink the other half and recall a dream." In the morning drink the remainder of the water with the affirmation "When I finish this water, I'll remember a dream." Lie still and see what you recall.

This method doesn't seem to be effective for everyone, but you'll never know if it's going to work for you until you try.

The Kinesthetic Cues Method

In *The Dream Workbook,* dream expert Dr. Jill Morris suggests the *kinesthetic cues method,* which relies on physical, body-positioning cues to prompt dream memory. By holding the same physical position you were in while you dreamed, there may be sufficient cues, what psychologists call *discriminative stimuli,* to trigger memories of your last dream.

This basic method is simple. When you wake up, either in the morning or at night, stay in bed with your eyes closed and hold the last position you were in while sleeping. Lie very still for a few moments, relax, and notice any feelings or images that may enter your mind. Just *allow* these symbols to emerge; don't try to force them.

Kinesthetic cues are more powerful than you might realize and are particularly valuable because they're often successful in prompting dream emotions. Once your body positioning helps you capture your dream feelings, the images usually follow.

You can, of course, use the affirmation technique and the kinesthetic cues method together by repeating affirmations at bedtime and practicing kinesthetic prompts when you wake.

The Skeptics' Method

Finally, if you're the ultimate skeptic and absolutely convinced that you *don't* dream, you might try the following:

Have your partner observe you as you sleep—that is, if you can talk him or her into staying awake. Your partner will need to watch you about two hours after you retire, so he or she can identify a REM period. Have your partner look carefully at your closed eyes, noticing when the jerky eye movements begin. When he or she can identify these rapid eye movements, have the person wake you gently. You'll be sound asleep, but without fail you'll remember a dream.

In fact, university laboratories that study dreams typically use a similar method. Subjects' physiologic activity such as brain waves, eye movements, and muscle tone are monitored and recorded on a polygraph. When subjects enter REM, they are awakened and asked to report any dream experiences.

How Do I Journal My Dreams?

It's impossible to overstate how important it is that you *record* your dreams. Journaling is the only surefire method for remembering dreams, as even the most dedicated dreamers will forget their dreams over the course of a busy day.

With practice you'll find yourself remembering more and more dreams until you get to the point where you easily recall a rich variety of dream experiences every night. Here are the five steps of successful dream journaling:

1. *Choose to remember your dreams.*

I can't overemphasize how important *attitude* is in remembering dreams. Most novice dreamers find that once they make the conscious decision, "I choose to remember my dreams," doing so seems to come naturally.

2. *Develop the habit of keeping a journal.*

Like it or not, we're creatures of habit, so dream journaling is most successful when we make it a part of our daily routine. Try to write down *something* every day.

3. *Write down your dreams as close to waking as possible.*

Given most people's busy lives, it's not always realistic to record dreams first thing in the morning, but try to do this as often as possible. *Keep a notepad and pen by your bedside.* Or keep a notebook computer by your bed and enter your dreams directly into your *DreamScape* journal.

4. *Keep your record brief.*

It's not necessary to record every small detail of your dream when you journal, particularly if, like most of us, you're pressed for time in the mornings. *Trying to do too much often results in doing nothing.* A few significant cues such as a strong dream feeling or a vivid image are usually enough. The rule of thumb is that your summary be sufficient to prompt recall of your dream experience at a later date.

Record anything about your dream—ideas, impressions, images, feelings, key symbols, whatever stands out to you even if they seem to be incomplete thoughts. And don't worry about being grammatically correct; it's not necessary to write complete sentences.

Include personal notes that will help put your dream in context, such as where you were sleeping if not at home or what important events were occurring in your waking life at the time. Finally, date and title your entry.

5. *Take advantage of your* DreamScape *journal.*

DreamScape includes a sophisticated electronic journal that allows you to catalog your dreams in a way not possible using pen and paper. Much more than a written diary, your *DreamScape* journal offers powerful search capabilities—find any symbol or group of symbols across hundreds of dreams, organize your dreams, and make personal notes about them. Even if you initially jot down your dreams in a notepad, transfer them to your *DreamScape* journal when you're able.

Once your dream has been entered into your *DreamScape* journal, you can transfer it to your *DreamScape* program with a single mouse click, allowing you to analyze at your convenience.

Simple, step-by-step instructions for using your *DreamScape* electronic journal can be found in appendix 2 of this book.

APPENDIX TWO

How to Use the DreamScape *Software*

One of my most important goals in designing *DreamScape* was to make the software easy to use. After all, a computer is just a tool, and any well-designed tool is effortless to use. Your time with *DreamScape* should be spent exploring the power of your dreams, not puzzling over the peculiarities of a computer.

Therefore someone with little or even no previous computer experience should find *DreamScape* easy to use. This appendix will give you simple, step-by-step instructions for installing and running the *DreamScape* program and journal on your PC.

This appendix will also provide a quick introduction to *how dream analysis is done on a computer*—so even if you're a computer expert, you may want to glance through the second half of this section.

Can My Computer Run DreamScape?

To use *DreamScape,* your computer will need the following:

- 386 or better PC
- Microsoft Windows 3.1 or Windows 95 or higher
- Hard drive with at least 5 MB free

180

- CD-ROM drive
- Mouse
- Minimum 8 MB of RAM

You must have *Microsoft Windows 3.1* or *Windows 95* installed in order to use *DreamScape.* You should have at least 8 MB of RAM. *DreamScape* requires about 5 MB of hard drive disk space and, of course, grows as you store dreams in your journal.

How Do I Install My DreamScape *Software?*

The *DreamScape* software comes on a CD-ROM. Installing is easy; here's what you should do:

- *STEP 1:*

  Insert the *DreamScape* CD-ROM.

  If you are using Windows 3.1, type *d:setup* (or use whatever letter designates your CD-ROM drive) from the Program Manager's File menu.

  If you are using Windows 95, click *Start,* then click *Run* and type *d:setup* (or use whatever letter designates your CD-ROM drive).

- *STEP 2:*

  Follow the instructions on the screen. Installation will take just a minute or so.

- *STEP 3:*

  DreamScape is installed and ready to use.

  In Windows 3.1, begin by double-clicking on the *DreamScape* or *DreamScape Journal* icon in the Program Manager.

  In Windows 95, click *Start,* click *Programs,* click *DreamScape,* then click either *DreamScape* or *DreamScape Journal.*

How Do I Use My DreamScape Software?

The first time you run *DreamScape*, you'll need to personalize it. When you see the screen that asks you to type in your name, put in a single name—*whatever name you like to be called*—this will most likely be your first name, but it could also be a nickname.

For example, "Jamie Jones" would probably want to type in *Jamie*. "Bernard W. Barnsworth Jr.," who calls himself "Barney," would type in *Barney*.

The name you choose to enter is very important—it's how *DreamScape* will address you. You'll need to enter your name only once—the first time you use the program; *DreamScape* will remember it. Once a name is entered, it's permanent and cannot be changed.

Once *DreamScape* is personalized, you're ready to enter your first dream. You'll automatically see *DreamScape's* nighttime scene—click on the *DreamScape* icon to continue on. You're then given the choice of *entering a dream or viewing the instructions*. Here's what these choices do:

♦ **Entering a dream.**
   To enter a dream, click *Dream. DreamScape* allows you to enter your dream in a couple of different ways. More about this later.

♦ **Step-by-step instructions.**
   This button accesses the instructions for using your *DreamScape* software—a shortened version of what you are reading here. You can get to this information by clicking the Help icon anywhere in the program.

Entering Your Dream

You may enter your dream as a *narrative*—a written summary of the dream—by typing out an entire dream or dream fragment.

This is often helpful in clarifying a vague dream, but try to be as brief as you can. As you know by now, your dream's *plot, characters, and situations* are not as important as the *feelings and impressions* that it leaves you.

If you wish, you may also enter your dream as a collection of symbols and emotions instead of a narrative. Don't be concerned with how the symbols tie together logically—*DreamScape* will do the work for you. Grammar and punctuation are also irrelevant—you don't even need to include them—*but spelling is very important.*

If you have already typed your dream elsewhere, such as in your *DreamScape* journal or a word-processing program, you may *paste* your dream into your *DreamScape* program by clicking the *Paste Dream From Journal* button.

Click the *New Dream* button if you wish to start over—that is, to erase whatever you've entered and type in a new dream.

Once you've finished entering your dream, click *Select Aspects.*

Choosing Your Aspects

You'll then be prompted to choose your *primary aspect.* The primary aspect is any symbol or dream emotion that stands out as more prominent or important than anything else in the dream.

To choose a primary aspect, simply click on the word you've chosen. *DreamScape* will tell you whether or not it's acceptable and able to be analyzed.

If your chosen primary aspect is able to be analyzed, you'll then be prompted to choose any additional symbols or emotions that you feel should be included. These are called *secondary aspects*—and they are symbols or dream emotions that you sense are important but not as prominent as the primary aspect.

Secondary aspects are optional; some dreams will have several, other dreams will have none—it's up to you to decide which dream aspects should be included. For some dreams, *DreamScape* also limits the number of secondary aspects you may enter to prevent your interpretation from becoming too complex.

For example, suppose you entered the following dream:

I was climbing the spiral staircase of a church tower. As I climbed, I could hear a bell above me. When I reached the top, I saw a beautiful kite soaring so near the tower I thought I could touch it. I was feeling exhilarated. . . .

Your first decision is to choose its *primary aspect*. Is this the *kite?* Or the *tower?* The *climb?* Or the feeling of *exhilaration?* Use your intuition to decide which symbol in your dream stands out as most prominent, and choose this as your primary aspect.

Next, are there any *secondary aspects* that your intuition tells you should be included? The *bell,* perhaps?

Once you've chosen all your aspects, you are ready to analyze your dream.

If you wish to change or add anything to your dream, click *Enter/ Edit Dream.* Then insert the cursor wherever you wish, click, and type your changes. If you wish to change all of your chosen aspects, click *Clear Aspects.*

What If My Primary Aspect Can't Be Analyzed?

If your Primary Aspect cannot be analyzed, you may *redo* your selection or *edit* your narrative.

Redoing simply means choosing a different primary aspect. You do this by clicking on a different word in the narrative summary. With this new click, the whole process begins again.

Editing allows you to type in new symbols or make whatever changes you'd like to your narrative. To do this, click *Enter/Edit Dream,* then click anywhere in the narrative where you wish to make changes, and type them in. When you're finished, click *Select Aspects.* You'll be prompted once again to choose your primary and secondary aspects.

Ready to Analyze

When you're completely finished with your narrative and have chosen your aspects, you are ready to interpret your dream. Click *Analyze Dream* and *DreamScape* will begin your interactive dream analysis.

Your DreamScape Software Is Interactive

DreamScape is an interactive analysis, which means that your *Dream-Scape* program will question you about the most important features of your dream as well as what might be going on in your life at the time—and then provide an interpretive response. In other words, your analysis is done in a kind of *question and answer* format.

This is the power of *DreamScape*—an *interactive* interpretation that is far superior to a static one, such as what you get from a dream dictionary. *DreamScape's* interactive analysis is able to furnish you with an *individualized* dream interpretation that considers your unique life circumstances.

The Four Icons

Navigating through *DreamScape* is done by clicking buttons on the screen. Most buttons are labeled and self-explanatory, such as *Yes, No, Continue,* and so forth.

In addition to labeled buttons, you'll often see *four icon buttons* on the right side of the screen. Click on these icons just as you would labeled buttons. Here's what these icon buttons do:

- **The Dream Catcher:**
  DreamScape's icon is a stylized dream catcher and provides *DreamScape's* credits.

- **The Question:**
  This icon brings up the on-line instructions as you require them.

- **The Book:**
  This icon opens your *DreamScape* journal.

- **The Stop Icon:**
  Clicking this icon button exits the program.

How Do I Use My DreamScape *Journal?*

Your *DreamScape* electronic journal is much more powerful than a handwritten diary. It is a place to store all of your dreams and offers powerful search and note-taking capabilities. It also allows you to easily transfer your dreams into the *DreamScape* program for analysis.

Installing Your DreamScape Journal

If you've installed your *DreamScape* program, then your journal is already installed in the same Program Manager File Group. If not, follow the simple installation instructions provided earlier.

Entering a Dream

When you open your *DreamScape* journal you'll see the title page and four icon buttons. Here's what these buttons do:

- Create a new entry in your journal.
- Take you to the first page of your journal.
- Take you to the last page of your journal.
- Open your *Dream Log*. This is a list of all the dreams in your journal.

Since this is your first use of the journal, click the pen icon to create a page. You will be asked to provide a *title* for your dream. We don't often think of dreams as having titles, but they are very helpful in identifying specific dreams. Keep your title short, just a few words.

Then enter your dream in the *dream field* and make any notes in the *notes field*.

Searching for a Symbol or Phrase

Your journal can search every dream for any word or phrase you choose. Just click the *Find* icon and enter the search word or phrase. All references to this word are cataloged for you.

Marking a Page

Mark any page or pages of your journal for easy future reference. It's like an *electronic bookmark* that keeps track of your dreams using any organization you wish. To access this feature, click the *Mark* icon.

The Log Button

Whenever you enter a new dream in your journal, its title, time, and date are logged automatically. This *log* is like an electronic table of contents. Use it to see a listing of all your dreams as well as to navigate easily to any dream within your journal. To access this feature, click the *Dream Log* icon.

Entering a Password

If you wish, you can prevent your journal from being opened by anyone but you by selecting and installing a *password*. A password-protected journal cannot be opened without first entering the correct password.

To access this feature, click the *Password* icon and follow the instructions on your screen.

Analyzing a Dream

Once you've entered a dream in your journal you do not need to type it again in the *DreamScape* program. To analyze a dream, just click the *DreamScape* icon and *DreamScape* will be opened and your dream will be transferred. Follow the instructions on your screen.

What If I Have Problems with My Software?

If you run into problems installing or using your *DreamScape* program, you may contact me for assistance. Please use the contact information provided on the About the Author page at the back of the book. I can usually respond most quickly to e-mail for strictly technical support problems.

Questions About Dream Interpretation

In this section I will present some of the most frequently asked questions about using the *DreamScape* software.

Question: How do I deal with long, complex dreams?

Answer: Break up your dream into smaller *dream fragments* and analyze each of these fragments separately with its own primary and secondary aspects. Try to capture the feel of your dream without worrying about how the symbols tie together.

Don't think of your dream as one long story, from beginning to end, with each character playing a role in the plot. A dream need not make sense in terms of *plot* or *storyline*. Odd and confusing dreams are just as helpful and informative as the ones that seem more logical. Feel your dream and let *DreamScape* do the rest.

Question: How do I choose my primary and secondary aspects?

Answer: Take a moment and think about each of the different symbols in your dream—try *visualizing* them as you recall them. Note any emotional impressions, sensations, odd or otherwise significant features. *Choose the part of the visualization that stands out the most for you—any feeling or image—as your primary aspect.*

Next, visualize the scene again, concentrating on the remaining symbols. If any of these somehow feel important, as if they are part of the message of your dream, choose them as secondary aspects.

Question: What if my dream makes no sense—if it's just a collection of bizarre images?

Answer: It's perfectly normal for a dream to appear as a series of seemingly nonsensical images. As I said earlier, don't think of the dream as one long story, from beginning to end, with each character playing a role in the plot. Just enter your dream symbols and let *DreamScape* do the work of making sense of them.

Question: I never remember my dreams. Do I dream?

Answer: Yes, everyone dreams, every night—in fact, it's impossible *not* to dream. But it's also not unusual to have some difficulty remembering your dreams. Dream recall is mostly about *habit*—once you're in the habit of remembering your dreams, you will in rich detail.

If you're having trouble, try using some of the dream recall strategies discussed in appendix 1. With practice you'll begin to remember some dreams in as soon as a week.

Question: What if my *DreamScape* analysis seems odd, contradictory, or doesn't make sense?

Answer: This is bound to happen on occasion. First try reanalyzing your dream several times, using a different primary aspect and different symbol combinations. If your interpretation still doesn't seem to fit, don't worry. Think on it for a few days, putting it on the back burner, and let your intuition work on it. Dreams usually precede conscious awareness in telling us about ourselves—in some instances you may not be ready to *hear* or understand the interpretation. Watch for any additional dream symbols that may help clarify the message. If you listen carefully, your dreams will eventually yield their secrets.

APPENDIX THREE

DreamScape *Affirmations*

Balance and harmony in life:

I seek balance in my life.
What changes can I make to bring the scales more in balance?
I am in a state of harmony and balance.

Communication:

I am open to the message being told me.
I am free to hear what is being said.
I seek honest and truthful communication.

Creativity:

I allow myself to see this situation from different perspectives.
I am free to explore new ideas and perspectives.
I release any need to judge or evaluate.

Decision making:

I allow myself to explore the possibilities for this decision.
I allow myself to find a solution.
I am open to guidance for my choice.

Energy and perseverance:

I create my reality of prosperity through the power of my dreams.
I affirm my desire and release my need for an outcome.
I flow with the natural order, allowing prosperity to engulf me.
I pass on my prosperity.
I allow myself to realize my true ambitions.
I am responsible in my desires.
I am aware of my needs and desires, but not obsessed by them.
I follow sensible actions and beliefs.

Faith and peace:

I think and act deliberately rather than from past fear.
I have the ability to enjoy each moment.
I have no interest in judging myself or others.
I have no interest in conflict.
I am connected with the spirit.
I allow my life to unfold, rather than manipulate.

Friendship:

I am free to explore new friendships.
I have much to offer, I am a desirable friend.
There are people who enjoy being with me.
I give myself permission to trust a friend.

Healing:

I am building a strong and invincible immune system.
My strength is growing through the power of my dreams.
My strength and healing powers are unlimited.
My dreams affirm my body's healthful state.

Healing (questions):

What shall I do to enhance my healing?
How can I get well?
Am I ready to resume my regular activities?

What is the condition of my body?
How do I strengthen my body and my immune system?

Healing (requests):

Please bring me comfort.
Please bring me peace and tranquillity.
Please bring me relief from pain.
Please bring me hope.

Intuition and prophecy:

I appreciate my intuitive abilities.
I am open to the guidance of my spiritual unconscious.
I trust my intuition.
I allow myself to retain the message of my dreams.
I allow my spiritual unconscious to emerge in my dreams.

Joy and happiness:

I allow myself to enjoy each moment.
I allow myself to be spontaneous, joyous, and cheerful.
I allow myself frequent, overwhelming episodes of appreciation.
I allow myself to connect with others and nature.
I allow my heart to smile.

Lucid dreaming:

I am free to be aware of being in my dreams.
I allow myself to become aware that I am dreaming.
Tonight I seek a lucid dream.
I am able to become aware while I dream.

Prosperity—guidance:

I allow myself to recognize the best path for my business actions.
I choose to increase my awareness of prosperity.
I allow myself to hear what my dreams are telling me.
I allow myself to recognize my true ambitions and desires.
I am aware of my needs and desires, but not obsessed by them.

Prosperity—incubating for success:

I am willing to accept success.
I seek fulfillment in all my professional endeavors.
I pass on my prosperity.
I accept that giving and receiving are part of the same circle.
I am responsible in my desires.

Relationships—how do I feel:

I am open to my feelings.
I accept my feelings as truthful and real.
How do I truly feel about my relationship?

Relationships—letting go:

When I am ready, I am able to let go of this relationship with love.
I wish to move ahead, leaving this relationship with love.
I seek strength and growth for myself.

Relationships—seeking connection with another:

I am open to a growing relationship.
I allow myself the joys of a healthy relationship.

Relationships—seeking understanding of another:

I am open to the message being told me.
I am free to hear what is being said.
I seek honest and truthful communication.

Self-esteem:

I love myself completely and without hesitation.
I practice self-love in my dream and waking realities.
I lovingly accept myself for who I am.

Self-love:

I allow myself to love myself.
I am free to love who I am.
I am a special person; there is no one in the universe like me.
God loves me unconditionally.

Spiritual growth:

I am open to the message of my dreams.
I allow my spiritual unconscious to emerge in my dreams.
I allow myself a connection with the spirit.
I seek the guidance of my Higher Self.

APPENDIX FOUR

Sample Dream Interpretations

Dream One

John is a twenty-two-year-old student who has been struggling with a decision to end a relationship or not. While this dilemma has been ongoing for some time, he was trying to *put it on the back burner* and avoid dealing with it at the time of this dream.

> I was climbing along a stony path on a hillside. When I finally got to the bottom of the hill, I realized I was in the middle of a cemetery and it was late at night. I was standing there feeling very afraid when suddenly a light appeared in the distance. . . .

DreamScape: Psychologically, roadways or paths symbolize choices and decisions in life. This may reflect a recent decision you've made or one you're presently considering. The nature of the road in your dream represents your feelings in the matter. For instance, a straight road indicates a clear choice with few distractions. A branching road suggests indecision. A rough or rocky road symbolizes some anguish over this choice.

Consider the roadway or path in this dream. Did something in your dream hinder forward progress?

John: Yes.

DreamScape: You may feel as if something or someone is blocking your path, John. This likely refers to your own feelings of uncertainty and indecision in some matter. Be sure of the road you're on before continuing—confidence will help steer you around the obstacles.

Climbing symbolizes emotional and intellectual growth. The direction of the climb in your dream is important. Think about the dream image—was the movement in an upward direction?

John: No.

DreamScape: Climbing down indicates a somewhat poor choice of direction. A stationary position suggests vacillation. Relate this to some aspect of your waking life—you might want to reconsider your path.

Don't take the death symbol in this dream literally, John. Instead look to its symbolic meaning. In this case, your image is concerned with feeling disconnected—have you felt in touch with your emotions lately?

John: No.

DreamScape: Take care not to bury your feelings, John. Your emotions, channeled properly, bring you power. Don't let negativity and fear deaden your feelings and responses.

The shadows or night symbol in your dream mean that you're not seeing clearly or are exploring unknown parts of your personality. Metaphorically you're groping around in the emotional darkness. Was there any fear or apprehensiveness associated with this dream image?

John: Yes.

DreamScape: It always seems fearful when you can see only part of a picture. Don't worry, though. When you're ready, you will recognize what's been hidden from your psychological view. There was a symbol of light in your dream—was this light dim or flickering?

John: Yes.

DreamScape: A dim or flickering light suggests confusion and difficulty in trusting your instincts. You may be distracted, with your attention scattered over too many unimportant matters. Step back, take some time to refocus and put this situation in a different light.

Your dream analysis is complete. Pleasant dreams, John.

Dream Two

Frank is a fifty-year-old co-owner of a small but successful business. Lately he has been concerned that his partner has been taking advantage of him—but has been reluctant to deal with the situation.

I was walking through a tunnel with my business partner. Suddenly we both fell off a cliff into a deep canyon. My partner started to yell wildly, accusing me for the fall. . . .

DreamScape: This dream represents a subconscious message cautioning you to examine the direction you've taken in some matter, Frank. It suggests a need to check your true feelings to see if you're using common sense and following your intuition. Are you concerned about the reliability of someone you depend on?

Frank: Yes.

DreamScape: Subterranean symbols such as tunnels or caves represent your suspicions of another. Perhaps you're concerned there's a hidden agenda at work. Look beyond surface explanations for actions that seem unusual or out of character. If you're uncomfortable with their performance or motives, assert yourself, Frank, don't cave in.

Think back on the image of the valley or canyon in your dream. Did this pit appear very deep?

Frank: Yes.

DreamScape: The depth of the image symbolizes the level of your concerns. Reconsider your path, Frank—use all your resources to investigate alternatives. Draw upon your intuition before proceeding. Don't continue blindly—it may be difficult to get out of a deep situation once you're in it.

With respect to the blaming or teasing in your dream, Frank, were the comments made in jest?

Frank: No.

DreamScape: You may be feeling cheated or taken advantage of. Alternatively, you may be feeling guilty for taking advantage of someone else. Examine your behavior and feelings in some recent interaction. Recall the scream or shriek in your dream—did you understand the intent of this yell?

Frank: Yes.

DreamScape: Good. Screaming or yelling in a dream means your subconscious is trying to get your attention. If you're able to relate the meaning of this symbol to some aspect of your waking life, then do so. If need be, examine your daily routines and look for guidance in other dream images.

The fall in your dream may represent a fear of losing control, as a recovering addict may fall off the wagon. Was there a flying or floating sensation in this dream?

Frank: No.

DreamScape: Then this dream may indicate some indecision on your part. Indecision is almost always manifested in dream symbols one way or another. Check to see if the barrier is self-imposed—as is usually the case—or if you're being limited from the outside. Have your energies been consumed by concerns about others lately?

Frank: Yes.

DreamScape: Your dream is telling you in no uncertain terms to recognize your own needs—and to act on them without delay. You cannot maintain your own personal strength and success if your basic psychological and emotional requirements have not been met.

Your dream analysis is complete. Pleasant dreams, Frank.

Dream Three

Mary is a thirty-three-year-old secretary whose dream reminded her of a long-standing goal to attend to her spiritual needs.

> I keep having this dream that I'm dreaming. Nothing really happens in my dream except I'm standing on a staircase. But I know it's all a dream. . . .

DreamScape: Your dream suggests a need for some quiet time—to put yourself into an introspective mode. Search inward for clarification—not for any immediate problem, but to reevaluate old beliefs and attitudes. This is a healthy process, Mary, one that encourages growth.

Have symbols or themes in this dream been recurring over the previous few weeks?

Mary: Yes.

DreamScape: Your subconscious is gently urging you forward toward personal growth, Mary. Growth cannot occur without change, and change consists of discarding old habits and beliefs. This is the process of open-minded self-discovery.

Dreams of dreaming are not at all unusual, Mary. Do you feel this dream within your dream was guiding you?

Mary: No.

DreamScape: You may be searching for greater inner understanding, Mary—but feel lost or without a guide. Self-understanding and growth are rewarding goals. Seek out whatever persons or tools you feel will help with your search—but ultimately, always follow your own heart and common sense.

Recall the stairs in your dream—were they rickety or uneven?

Mary: Yes.

DreamScape: Images of stairs or steps have strong spiritual symbolism. The unsteadiness of your dream image symbolizes how you view your spiritual journey. It may be time to attend to your spiritual needs, Mary. Choose a path where you feel most comfortable—where the footing is solid.

Your dream analysis is complete. Pleasant dreams, Mary.

Dream Four

Michael is an eighteen-year-old college freshman living away from home for the first time in order to go to school. His dream points out the self-consciousness and interpersonal anxiety associated with going away to school and how much he really misses home.

> In my dream I am walking around my house wearing a knight's armor. Every door I try to go in is either locked or blocked by chairs piled up. . . .

DreamScape: Your dream represents feelings of vulnerability—a desire for psychological refuge. Jungian psychology teaches us that we often hide behind a barrier of self-protection called the persona. This is how you allow others to see you—the outer appearance or mask you present to the world. You may be feeling as though your persona is not covering you completely—as if a part of you is exposed. Have you felt a need to gloss over something or put on appearances?

Michael: Yes.

DreamScape: Your dream reflects a need for psychological armor or shielding, Michael. Perhaps you've been less than completely honest about your true feelings with someone. Or you're sensing some insecurity or uncertainty about a relationship. Honestly ask yourself what it is you're trying to protect.

The house in your dream refers to yourself—subconscious attitudes toward your body, mind, and spirit. The interior of the house symbolizes psychological and physical function. For instance, a library or study represents mental abilities; a bathroom, the cleansing of old ideas and feelings; the bedroom, sexuality or rest; and the living room, interpersonal skills. Was the house in your dream a place you'd like to live?

Michael: Yes.

DreamScape: Then interpret the house symbolism in your dream as a desire for shelter, Michael. You may be seeking a refuge against a difficult day or even a period in your life, longing for the comfort and safety of home.

Barriers in dreams, such as walls or doorways, may be a damming up of undesirable feelings, Michael. Have you been able to display your emotions openly and spontaneously?

Michael: No.

DreamScape: Then interpret the barrier in your dream as defensiveness that may be obstructing personal growth and understanding, particularly within a relationship. Don't fear your emotions, Michael, channel and use them appropriately.

Your dream analysis is complete. Pleasant dreams, Michael.

Dream Five

Pat is a forty-three-year-old woman who was going through a divorce at the time of this dream. She felt cheated but helpless to stand up to her powerful husband.

> I was alone in a boat, holding a big knife. Then the boat started to sink. I was able to jump out of the boat just as it went under. But for some reason, I held on tightly to the knife the whole time. . . .

DreamScape: Your dream suggests two opposing forces—the stronger force oppressing the weaker. This may involve frustration or aggressiveness on your part or in someone around you. When this occurs, true feelings are inhibited and desired goals seldom reached. Did you try to prevent the boat from sinking?

Pat: Yes.

DreamScape: Feelings of powerlessness are symbolized in this dream, Pat. You may feel as though you're under pressure and just keeping your head above water—metaphorically feeling as if you must sink or swim. If this dream image persists, perhaps it's time to seek assistance from a trusted friend or counselor. Did someone or something in your dream jump or leap in order to escape danger?

Pat: Yes.

DreamScape: Then interpret this as an attempt to gain greater control over some aspect of your life, Pat. The jump symbolizes a desire to leap ahead psychologically, even in the face of uncertainty—a leap of faith. That the jump was done to escape danger suggests this need for control is strong or building inside you. Trust your intuition in this matter. Have you been angry with someone lately, Pat?

Pat: Yes.

DreamScape: Then interpret the knife in your dream as reflecting feelings of frustration over a personal relationship. The more lethal the weapon symbol, the deeper you feel this frustration.

As the demands and rigors of daily living take their toll, we often use the dream state as a pressure valve to safely isolate ourselves from unexpressed emotions. Dreams of solitude are common when we feel overtaxed in relationships, Pat. Do you feel others have been making unreasonable demands of you lately?

Pat: Yes.

DreamScape: Your dream images are reflecting the desire for refuge from the demands of your life, Pat. Be assertive with respect to your own needs and desires. Respect the rights of others, but at the same time demand the same respect for yourself.

Your dream analysis is complete. Pleasant dreams, Pat.

Dream Six

Nichole is a thirty-eight-year-old systems analyst who, at the time of this dream, was considering leaving a secure but unchallenging position and starting her own consulting business.

> All I can remember is that I was driving my car to the airport. I was late, but it didn't seem to matter—I knew the plane wouldn't leave without me because I was the pilot. . . .

DreamScape: Vehicles symbolize your journey through business or educational matters. In all likelihood this means that you're preoccupied with some business dealing or perhaps taking advantage of opportunities being presented. Think about the road you're taking, Nichole. Your drive and ambition are the means of getting you to your chosen destination.

Recall the vehicle symbolized in your dream—were you responsible for its direction?

Nichole: Yes.

DreamScape: Interpret this in the context of some current business or educational matter—you're steering and directing a problem or project, or it's time for you to do so. The symbolism suggests your confidence in this matter is high, Nichole—and such confidence often results in a lucrative and successful outcome.

Themes of travel represent new ideas and change. Did the traveling occur at a fast rate of speed?

Nichole: Yes.

DreamScape: Great. The rate of travel mirrors your potential for action, Nichole. The faster you move in a dream journey and the more control you feel during the trip, the more promising your efforts are in some matter. Are you considering a new business venture or a change in academic study?

Nichole: Yes.

DreamScape: Psychologically you're in the depot or airport, Nichole. In other words, you're at a decision point—a choice regarding your direction and destination. The details and emotional tone of your dream can give you insight into your true feelings and intuition about this new venture. A positive tone reflects a favorable attitude.

This dream raises questions about the direction you feel you're heading in some aspect of your life. Has someone been trying to convince you of something or influence a decision?

Nichole: No.

DreamScape: Your dream indicates a desire to take over the helm and assume greater control over some aspect of your life. While it may seem easier to allow others to make decisions for you, ultimately your happiness follows your own actions.

Your dream analysis is complete. Pleasant dreams, Nichole.

SELECTED BIBLIOGRAPHY

DreamScape's research drew from a diverse variety of contemporary and historical cultural dream systems. Here is a sample of some interesting readings of varying levels of complexity.

Adler, A. 1932. *The practice and theory of individual psychology.* London: Routledge & Kegan Paul, Ltd.

Adler, G. 1967. *Studies in analytical psychology.* New York: G. P. Putnam's Sons.

Campbell, J. 1959. *The masks of god: Primitive mythology.* New York: Viking Press.

———. 1962. *The masks of god: Oriental mythology.* New York: Viking Press.

Cirlot, J. E. 1971. *A dictionary of symbols.* New York: Philosophical Library.

Cohen, D. 1979. *Sleep and dreaming: Origins, nature, and functions.* New York: Pergamon Press.

Cooper, J. C. 1982. *Symbolism: The universal language.* Wellingborough, Northhamptonshire, U.K.: Aquarian Press.

Crisp, T. 1990. *Dream dictionary: A guide to dream and sleep experiences.* New York: Dell Publishing.

Delaney, G. 1994. *Sexual dreams.* New York: Fawcett.

Dement, W. 1972. *Some must watch while some must sleep.* San Francisco: W. H. Freeman.

DeMallie, R. J., and D. R. Parks. 1987. *Sioux Indian religion: Tradition and innovation.* Norman, Okla.: University of Oklahoma Press.

Fanning, P. 1988. *Visualization for change.* Oakland, Calif.: New Harbinger Publications.

Ferm, V. 1959. *American superstitions.* New York: Philosophical Library.

Fine, R. 1979. *A history of psychoanalysis.* New York: Columbia University Press.

Fosshage, J. L., and C. A. Loew. 1978. *Dream interpretation: A comparative study.* New York: S. P. Medical & Scientific Books.

Foulkes, D. 1978. *A grammar of dreams.* New York: Basic Books.

Fromm, E. 1951. *The forgotten language.* New York: Grove Press.

Gackenbach, J. 1986. *Sleep and dreams.* New York: Garland Publishing.

Garfield, P. 1991. *The healing power of dreams.* New York: Fireside.

———. 1995. *Creative dreaming, 2E.* New York: Fireside.

Goldenweiser, A. 1965. *History, psychology and culture.* Gloucester, Mass.: Peter Smith.

Hall, J. A. 1977. *Clinical uses of dreams: Jungian interpretations and enactments.* New York: Grune & Stratton.

Hobson, A. 1985. *The dreaming brain.* New York: Basic Books.

Hook, R. H. 1979. *Fantasy and symbols.* New York: Academic Press.

Howitt, M. 1970. *The history of magic.* New York: New York University Press.

Jobes, G. 1962. *Dictionary of mythology, folklore, and symbols.* New York: Scarecrow Press.

Jung, C. G. 1963. *Psychology of the unconscious.* New York: Dodd, Mead & Company.

———. 1964. *Man and his symbols.* New York: Doubleday & Company.

Koren, H. J. 1955. *An introduction to the philosophy of animate nature.* St. Louis: B. Herder Company.

Kramer, M. 1969. *Dream psychology and the new biology of dreaming.* Springfield, Ill.: Charles C. Thomas Publisher.

Laszlo, V. S. 1959. *The basic writings of C. G. Jung.* New York: The Modern Library.

Leaf, M. J. 1979. *Mind, man and science.* New York: Columbia University Press.

Legge, J., trans. 1973. *I Ching: Book of changes*. New York: Causeway Books.

Lewis, I. 1977. *Symbols and sentiments: Cross-cultural studies in symbolism*. New York: Academic Press.

Lewis, J. 1995. *The dream encyclopedia*. Detroit: Visible Ink Press.

Matthews, B. 1986. *The Herder symbol dictionary*. Wilmette, Ill.: Chiron Publications.

McGuire, W., ed. 1984. *Dream analysis: Notes on a seminar given in 1928–1930 by C. G. Jung*. Princeton, N.J.: Princeton University Press.

Morris, J. 1985. *The dream workbook*. New York: Fawcett Crest.

Opie, I., and M. Tatem. 1989. *A dictionary of superstitions*. New York: Oxford University Press.

Parman, S. 1991. *Dream and culture: An anthropological study of the western intellectual tradition*. New York: Praeger.

Perls, F. S. 1969. *Gestalt therapy verbatim*. Lafayette, Calif.: Real People Press.

Siegel, B. 1989. *Peace, love and healing*. New York: Harper & Row.

Singer, J. L., and K. S. Pope. 1978. *The power of human imagination*. New York: Plenum Press.

Tedlock, B. 1987. *Dreaming: Anthropological and psychological interpretations*. New York: Cambridge University Press.

Thass-Thienemann, T. 1973. *The interpretation of language*. New York: Jason Aronson.

Van de Castle, R. 1994. *Our dreaming mind*. New York: Ballantine Books.

Vogel, V. L. 1970. *American Indian medicine*. Norman, Okla.: University of Oklahoma Press.

Watts, A. 1972. *The book: On the taboo of knowing who you are*. New York: Vintage Books.

———. 1973. *This is it*. New York: Vintage Books.

Wolff, W. 1952. *The dream: Mirror of consciousness*. Westport, Conn.: Greenwood Press.

Woods, R. 1947. *The world of dreams*. New York: Random House.

Yamamoto, G. K. 1988. *Creative dream analysis*. Tucson, Ariz.: Harbinger House.

ASPECT INDEX

This index contains the most commonly experienced dream symbols and emotions, together referred to as *aspects*. Using the *DreamScape* method, these aspects are classified into the emotional themes that constitute dream reality and give symbolism its power. Use these symbols as a guide, recognizing that each dream is unique and personal.

To use this index, find your *primary aspect* (the symbol or dream emotion most prominent in your dream) listed alphabetically in the list that follows. Beside each aspect is the theme or themes with which this symbol or emotion is most commonly associated, as well as the page numbers where you'll find this theme described. For example, the symbols *angel, heaven,* and *church* are all associated with themes of *sacredness*. Aspects that are also theme titles are followed only by page numbers.

Because dream symbolism is different for each of us, many themes are discussed in more than one chapter. For instance, *cloud* is associated with *faith (soul)* as well as *opportunity (prosperity),* so there are entries for this theme in both chapters. Choose whichever sections seem most appropriate given the feelings and impressions of your specific dream.

castle, *body,* 66; *wealth,* 123
cat, *emotion,* 37; *friendship,* 91
catacomb, *transformation,* 148
cathedral, *body,* 66; *sacredness,* 147
cave, *control,* 33
ceiling, *vulnerability,* 44
celebration, *joy,* 68; *loneliness,* 92
celebrity, *loneliness,* 92; *need,* 95;
    self-esteem, 42; *vulnerability,* 44
celibate, *sex,* 97
cellar, *body,* 66
cemetery, *transformation,* 148
champion, *opportunity,* 121; *vulnerability,*
    44
change, *communication,* 88; *stress,* 95;
    transformation, 148
chapel, *sacredness,* 147
charity, *friendship,* 91; *love,* 94
chart, *communication,* 88; *intuition,* 168
chase, *choice,* 115; *control,* 33; *need,* 95;
    self-esteem, 44; *stress,* 71; *vulnerability,*
    44
cheer, *joy,* 68
child, *innocence,* 143
childbirth, *transformation,* 148
chime, *love,* 94
chimney, *body,* 68
chimpanzee, *work,* 125
choice, 115
choking, *anger,* 63; *balance,* 65; *body,* 66;
    control, 33; *criticism,* 36; *need,* 95; *risk,*
    70; *self-esteem,* 42; *stress,* 71;
    vulnerability, 44
chop, *loss,* 44; *stress,* 71
Christ, *sacredness,* 147
Christmas, *innocence,* 143; *loneliness,* 92;
    sacredness, 147
church, *sacredness,* 147
cinema, *self-esteem,* 42; *vulnerability,* 44
circus, *emotion,* 37; *joy,* 68; *loneliness,* 92;
    need, 95; *vulnerability,* 44
clairvoyance, 166
classroom, *communication,* 88; *intellect,*
    119
claw, *control,* 33
clay, *intuition,* 168
cleaning, *choice,* 115; *emotion,* 37;
    friendship, 91; *need,* 95; *transformation,*
    148
cliff, *choice,* 115; *opportunity,* 121; *risk,*
    70
climbing, *choice,* 115; *opportunity,* 121;
    risk, 70; *inspiration,* 145; *intuition,* 174
clock, *transformation,* 148
closet, *body,* 68; *emotion,* 37

clothing, *stress,* 71; *vulnerability,* 44
cloud, *faith,* 142; *friendship,* 91;
    inspiration, 145; *intuition,* 168;
    opportunity, 121; *transformation,* 148
clown, *innocence,* 143; *joy,* 68
coach, *control,* 33; *criticism,* 36
coal, *energy,* 117
coat, *stress,* 71; *vulnerability,* 44
code, *communication,* 88
coffin, *transformation,* 148
coin, *wealth,* 122
cold, *risk,* 70
college, *intellect,* 119
colon, *body,* 66; *emotion,* 37
color, *anger,* 63; *emotion,* 37; *energy,* 117;
    faith, 142; *intellect,* 119; *intuition,* 168
comb, *body,* 66; *self-esteem,* 42;
    vulnerability, 44
combat, *anger,* 63; *communication,* 88;
    criticism, 36; *stress,* 71; *vulnerability,* 44
comedian, *joy,* 68
comedy, *joy,* 68
communication, 88
companion, *friendship,* 91
compass, *communication,* 88; *intuition,*
    168
compassion, *love,* 94
complexion, *body,* 66
compulsion, *risk,* 70; *stress,* 71;
    vulnerability, 44
computer, *communication,* 88; *intellect,*
    119
concealed, *loneliness,* 92
conceit, *loneliness,* 92; *need,* 95;
    self-esteem, 42; *vulnerability,* 44
condom, *risk,* 70; *sex,* 97
confetti, *love,* 94
confidence, *self-esteem,* 42
confinement, *control,* 33
confusion, *choice,* 115; *risk,* 70
construction, *body,* 66; *friendship,* 91;
    opportunity, 121; *self-esteem,* 42; *work,*
    125
container, *choice,* 115; *emotion,* 37;
    vulnerability, 44
contraception, *risk,* 70; *sex,* 97
control, 33
convict, *control,* 33; *risk,* 70;
    vulnerability, 44
coral, *water,* 151
corpse, *risk,* 70; *transformation,* 148
cosmetics, *sex,* 97; *self-esteem,* 42;
    vulnerability, 44
costume, *self-esteem,* 42; *vulnerability,* 44
counterfeit, *vulnerability,* 44; *wealth,* 122

country, *communication*, 88; *control*, 33; *loneliness*, 92; *opportunity*, 121; *vulnerability*, 44
courage, *energy*, 117
court, *balance*, 65
cover, *vulnerability*, 44
cow, *work*, 125
coward, *emotion*, 37; *need*, 95; *self-esteem*, 42; *stress*, 71; *vulnerability*, 44
crack, *communication*, 88; *stress*, 71; *transformation*, 148
cradle, *innocence*, 143; *transformation*, 148
crate, *choice*, 115; *emotion*, 37; *vulnerability*, 44
crater, *choice*, 115
creation, *faith*, 142; *transformation*, 148; *water*, 151
crib, *innocence*, 143; *transformation*, 148
crime, *risk*, 70; *wealth*, 122
cripple, *body*, 66; *risk*, 70; *intellect*, 119; *intuition*, 168; *self-esteem*, 42
criticism, 36
crocodile, *emotion*, 37; *magic*, 169
cross, *sacredness*, 147; *transformation*, 148
crow, *inspiration*, 145; *magic*, 169
crowd, *joy*, 68; *loneliness*, 92; *need*, 95; *vulnerability*, 44
crown, *communication*, 88; *control*, 33; *criticism*, 36; *self-esteem*, 42; *vulnerability*, 44; wealth, 122
crutch, *body*, 66; *risk*, 70; *self-esteem*, 42
cry, *loneliness*, 92; *loss*, 41; *need*, 95
crypt, *magic*, 169; *transformation*, 148
cuddle, *friendship*, 91; *love*, 94
cult, *risk*, 70; *stress*, 71; *vulnerability*, 44
cupid, *love*, 94
cure, *balance*, 65; *body*, 66; *joy*, 68
currency, *wealth*, 122
cut, *loss*, 41; *stress*, 71

dam, *communication*, 88; *emotion*, 37; *opportunity*, 121; *stress*, 71; *vulnerability*, 44
dance, *joy*, 68
danger, *risk*, 70; *stress*, 71; *vulnerability*, 44
darkness, *control*, 33; *vulnerability*, 44
deaf, *body*, 66; communication, 88; *risk*, 70; *intellect*, 119; *intuition*, 168; *self-esteem*, 42
death, *clairvoyance*, 166; *intuition*, 168; *transformation*, 148
debt, *wealth*, 122
deer, *emotion*, 37; *work*, 125

defeat, *loss*, 41
defecation, *emotion*, 37; *stress*, 71
defection, *control*, 33; *self-esteem*, 42
delight, *joy*, 68
demon, *magic*, 169; *risk*, 70
dentist, *body*, 67; *stress*, 71
dependency, *need*, 95
depression, *loneliness*, 92; *loss*, 41; *need*, 95
descend, *choice*, 115; *opportunity*, 121; *risk*, 70; *inspiration*, 145; *intuition*, 168
desert, *loneliness*, 92
destruction, *risk*, 70; *transformation*, 148
detective, *control*, 33; *emotion*, 37; *intuition*, 168
devil, *magic*, 169; *risk*, 70
diamond, *wealth*, 122
diary, *communication*, 88
dictionary, *communication*, 88; *intellect*, 119
diet, *body*, 66
digestion, *body*, 66; *stress*, 71
digging, *vulnerability*, 44
dime, *wealth*, 122
dinosaur, *transformation*, 148
diploma, *intellect*, 119; *opportunity*, 121; *vulnerability*, 44
direction, *choice*, 115; *intuition*, 168
disability, *body*, 66; *risk*, 70; *intellect*, 119; *intuition*, 168; *self-esteem*, 42
disappear, *loss*, 41; *self-esteem*, 42; *vulnerability*, 44
disaster, *emotion*, 37; *transformation*, 148
discovery, *intuition*, 168
disease, *body*, 66; *risk*, 70; *stress*, 71; *vulnerability*, 44
disguise, *self-esteem*, 42; *vulnerability*, 44
dish, *stress*, 71
dissolve, *loss*, 31; *self-esteem*, 42; *vulnerability*, 44
divine, *sacredness*, 147
divorce, *loneliness*, 92; *loss*, 41; *stress*, 71; *transformation*, 148
dock, *vulnerability*, 44
doctor, *body*, 66; *stress*, 71
dog, *friendship*, 91
dollar, *wealth*, 122
dolphin, *water*, 151
donkey, *emotion*, 37; *work*, 125
door, *opportunity*, 121
doubt, *self-esteem*, 42
dove, *faith*, 142; *innocence*, 146; *inspiration*, 145
dragon, *magic*, 169
drama, *self-esteem*, 42; *vulnerability*, 44

dream, *intuition*, 168
drinking, *risk*, 70; *stress*, 71; *vulnerability*, 44
driving, *choice*, 115
drowning, *anger*, 63; *balance*, 65; *body*, 66; *control*, 33; *criticism*, 36; *need*, 95; *risk*, 70; *self-esteem*, 42; *stress*, 71; *vulnerability*, 44
drugs, *risk*, 70
duck, *emotion*, 37; *work*, 125
duel, *anger*, 63; *communication*, 88; *criticism*, 36; *stress*, 71; *vulnerability*, 44
dung, *emotion*, 37; *stress*, 71
duty, *work*, 125

eagle, *inspiration*, 145
ear, *body*, 66; *intuition*, 168
earth, *intuition*, 168
earthquake, *emotion*, 37; *energy*, 117; *transformation*, 148
Easter, *innocence*, 143; *loneliness*, 92; *sacredness*, 147
eating, *choice*, 115; *stress*, 71; *vulnerability*, 44
education, *intellect*, 119; *opportunity*, 121
egg, *innocence*, 143; *transformation*, 148
ejaculate, *sex*, 97
electricity, *energy*, 117
elephant, *emotion*, 37; *work*, 125
elevator, *choice*, 115
elf, *magic*, 169
embarrassment, *self-esteem*, 42
embrace, *friendship*, 91; *love*, 94
emerald, *wealth*, 122
emergency, *risk*, 70; *stress*, 71; *vulnerability*, 44
emotion, 37
employee, *work*, 125
employer, *work*, 125
employment, *work*, 125
encyclopedia, *communication*, 88; *intellect*, 119
enemy, *risk*, 70; *stress*, 71; *vulnerability*, 44
energy, 117
engine, *energy*, 117
entertainment, *innocence*, 143; *joy*, 68
envelope, *communication*, 88
envy, *self-esteem*, 42; *vulnerability*, 44
erection, *body*, 66; *sex*, 97
erotic, *sex*, 97
escalator, *choice*, 115; *energy*, 117
escape, *control*, 33; *self-esteem*, 42
ESP, *clairvoyance*, 166
evil, *magic*, 169; *risk*, 70

examination, *criticism*, 36; *intellect*, 119; *stress*, 71; *vulnerability*, 44
excrement, *emotion*, 37; *stress*, 71
exercise, *balance*, 65; *stress*, 71
explorer, *intuition*, 168
explosives, *risk*, 70; *stress*, 71; *vulnerability*, 44
eye, *body*, 67; *intuition*, 168

face, *body*, 67
factory, *work*, 125
fade, *loss*, 41; *self-esteem*, 42; *vulnerability*, 44
failure, *loss*, 41; *self-esteem*, 42
fairy, *magic*, 169
faith, 142
falcon, *inspiration*, 145
falling, *control*, 33
family, *love*, 94; *need*, 95
fantasy, *sex*, 97
farm, *work*, 125
fat, *body*, 66; *risk*, 70
father, *love*, 94; *need*, 95
fatigue, *risk*, 70; *stress*, 71
fear, *emotion*, 37; *need*, 95; *stress*, 71; *vulnerability*, 44;
feces, *emotion*, 37; *stress*, 71
feelings, *emotion*, 37
fence, *communication*, 88; *stress*, 71; *vulnerability*, 44
fertilizer, *emotion*, 37; *stress*, 71
festival, *joy*, 68; *loneliness*, 92; *love*, 94; *need*, 95
feud, *anger*, 63; *communication*, 88; *risk*, 70
fever, *body*, 66; *risk*, 70; *stress*, 71; *vulnerability*, 44
fight, *anger*, 63; *communication*, 88; *criticism*, 36; *stress*, 71; *vulnerability*, 44
film, *communication*, 88; *self-esteem*, 42; *vulnerability*, 44
finding, *inspiration*, 145; *intuition*, 168
finger, *body*, 67
fire, *energy*, 117
fish, *water*, 151
flag, *vulnerability*, 44
flame, *energy*, 117
flattery, *loneliness*, 92; *need*, 95; *self-esteem*, 42; *vulnerability*, 44
flee, *control*, 33; *self-esteem*, 42
floating, *inspiration*, 145
flood, *water*, 151; *transformation*, 148
floor, *body*, 66
flower, *innocence*, 143; *love*, 94
flu, *stress*, 71

flying, *inspiration,* 145
fog, *choice,* 115; *intuition,* 168;
    opportunity, 121; *transformation,* 148
fondness, *love,* 94
food, *choice,* 115; *opportunity,* 121; *stress,*
    71; *vulnerability,* 44
foot, *body,* 67
foreplay, *sex,* 97
forest, *inspiration,* 145
forgiveness, *love,* 94
fortress, *vulnerability,* 44
fountain, *water,* 151
friend, *friendship,* 91
friendship, 91
fright, *emotion,* 37; *need,* 95; *stress,* 71;
    vulnerability, 44
frog, *emotion,* 37; *magic,* 169
frozen, *water,* 151
fruit, *choice,* 115; *inspiration,* 145;
    opportunity, 121
frustration, *anger,* 63
fuel, *energy,* 117
fun, *innocence,* 143; *joy,* 68
funeral, *transformation,* 148
funny, *joy,* 68
fur, *vulnerability,* 44
furniture, *body,* 66; *wealth,* 122

galaxy, *faith,* 142; *inspiration,* 145;
    intuition, 168
gambling, *risk,* 70
game, *innocence,* 143
garbage, *emotion,* 37
garden, *faith,* 142; *intuition,* 168;
    opportunity, 121
gasoline, *energy,* 117
gate, *opportunity,* 121
gavel, *balance,* 65
gem, *wealth,* 122
generator, *energy,* 117
genitals, *sex,* 97
genius, *intellect,* 119
geyser, *water,* 151
ghost, *magic,* 169
ghoul, *magic,* 169; *risk,* 70
giant, *magic,* 169; *risk,* 70; *vulnerability,*
    44
gift, *love,* 94
giggle, *joy,* 68
girl, *innocence,* 143
girlfriend, *friendship,* 91; *love,* 94
glacier, *water,* 151
glasses, *intuition,* 168
glider, *inspiration,* 145
gliding, *inspiration,* 145

glow, *love,* 94
gnat, *stress,* 71
goat, *emotion,* 37; *work,* 125
goddess, *magic,* 169
gold, *wealth,* 122
gopher, *emotion,* 37; *work,* 125
gorilla, *emotion,* 37; *work,* 125
graduation, *intellect,* 119; *vulnerability,* 44
gratitude, *love,* 94
grave, *transformation,* 148
graveyard, *transformation,* 148
grieve, *loneliness,* 92; *loss,* 41; *need,* 95
guard, *vulnerability,* 44
guilt, *emotion,* 37
gun, *control,* 33; *transformation,* 148
gymnasium, *balance,* 65; *stress,* 71

hair, *body,* 67; *vulnerability,* 44
hallway, *body,* 68
halo, *intuition,* 168; *sacredness,* 147
hammer, *work,* 125
hand, *body,* 67
happy, *joy,* 68
harassment, *criticism,* 36
harbor, *vulnerability,* 44
harvest, *transformation,* 148
hat, *stress,* 71; *vulnerability,* 44
hatchet, *intellect,* 119
hatred, *anger,* 63; *emotion,* 37; *risk,* 70
haunt, *magic,* 170
hawk, *inspiration,* 145
head, *body,* 67; *intellect,* 119
headache, *body,* 67; *stress,* 71
healer, *balance,* 65; *body,* 66; *joy,* 68
health, *balance,* 65; *body,* 66; *joy,* 68; *risk,*
    70; *stress,* 71
hearing, *body,* 67; *inspiration,* 145;
    intuition, 168
hearse, *transformation,* 148
heart, *body,* 67; *love,* 94
heartburn, *anger,* 63; *body,* 66; *risk,* 70;
    stress, 71
hearth, *energy,* 117
heat, *energy,* 117
heaven, *sacredness,* 147
hell, *magic,* 169; *risk,* 70
helm, *choice,* 115
helplessness, *need,* 95
hermit, *loneliness,* 92
hero, *need,* 95; *self-esteem,* 42
hidden, *loneliness,* 92
hill, *faith,* 141; *intuition,* 168; *opportunity,*
    121; *sacredness,* 147
hitting, *anger,* 63; *criticism,* 36; *stress,* 71;
    vulnerability, 44

hole, *balance*, 65; *risk*, 70; *vulnerability*, 44
holiday, *innocence*, 143; *loneliness*, 92
homosexuality, *sex*, 97
hopelessness, *vulnerability*, 44
horn, *risk*, 70
horoscope, *clairvoyance*, 166; *magic*, 169
horse, *emotion*, 37; *work*, 125
hospital, *body*, 66; *stress*, 71
hostage, *control*, 33; *risk*, 70; *vulnerability*,
    44
hostility, *anger*, 63
hotel, *body*, 67
house, *body*, 68
housework, *choice*, 115; *emotion*, 37;
    friendship, 91; *need*, 95; *transformation*,
    148
hug, *friendship*, 91; *love*, 94
humiliation, *self-esteem*, 42
humor, *joy*, 68
hunger, *body*, 66; *need*, 95; *stress*, 71
hunted, *choice*, 115; *control*, 36; *need*, 95;
    self-esteem, 42; *stress*, 71; *vulnerability*,
    44
hurricane, *emotion*, 37; *energy*, 117;
    transformation, 148
husband, *love*, 94; *need*, 95
hymn, *sacredness*, 147
hysterectomy, *loss*, 41; *risk*, 70; *stress*, 71

ice, *water*, 151
iceberg, *water*, 151
idol, *magic*, 169
illness, *body*, 66; *risk*, 70; *stress*, 71;
    vulnerability, 44
impotence, *sex*, 97
income, *wealth*, 122
indigestion, *anger*, 63; *body*, 66; *risk*, 70;
    stress, 71
infant, *innocence*, 143
infection, *body*, 66; *risk*, 70; *stress*, 71;
    vulnerability, 44
inheritance, *wealth*, 122
injection, *body*, 66; *risk*, 70; *stress*, 71
injury, *body*, 66; *stress*, 71
ink, *communication*, 88
innocence, 143
insanity, *magic*, 169; *risk*, 70
insect, *stress*, 71
insecurity, *need*, 95; *vulnerability*, 44
inspiration, 145
instinct, *intuition*, 168
insurance, *vulnerability*, 44; *wealth*, 122
intellect, 119
intercourse, *sex*, 97
intestine, *body*, 67

intuition, 168
investment, *wealth*, 122
invisible, *loss*, 41; *self-esteem*, 42;
    vulnerability, 44
irritation, *anger*, 63
island, *loneliness*, 92

jacket, *stress*, 71; *vulnerability*, 44
jail, *control*, 33; *risk*, 70; *vulnerability*, 44
jar, *choice*, 115; *emotion*, 37; *vulnerability*,
    44
jealousy, *need*, 95
jet, *energy*, 117; *inspiration*, 145;
    opportunity, 121
jewelry, *sex*, 97; *self-esteem*, 42;
    vulnerability, 44; *wealth*, 122
jewels, *wealth*, 122
job, *work*, 125
joke, *joy*, 68
journal, *communication*, 88
journey, *choice*, 115
joy, 68
juggle, *balance*, 65
juggler, *innocence*, 143; *joy*, 68
jump, *choice*, 115
jungle, *emotion*, 37
jury, *balance*, 65; *control*, 33; *vulnerability*,
    44
justice, *balance*, 65

kangaroo, *emotion*, 37; *work*, 125
key, *communication*, 88
kidnap, *loss*, 41; *opportunity*, 121; *risk*,
    70; *vulnerability*, 44
kill, *control*, 33; *risk*, 70; *transformation*,
    148
king, *communication*, 88; *control*, 33;
    criticism, 36
kiss, *friendship*, 91; *love*, 94
kite, *inspiration*, 145
kitten, *emotion*, 37; *innocence*, 143
knife, *intellect*, 119; *risk*, 70
knitting, *communication*, 88
Koran, *sacredness*, 147

laboratory, *intellect*, 119
ladder, *faith*, 142; *inspiration*, 145;
    intuition, 168
lake, *water*, 151
lamb, *emotion*, 37; *work*, 125
lame, *body*, 66; *risk*, 70; *intellect*, 119;
    intuition, 168; *self-esteem*, 42
language, *communication*, 88
lantern, *intellect*, 119; *intuition*, 168
laser, *energy*, 117

laughter, *joy*, 68
laundry, *choice*, 115; *emotion*, 37;
 friendship, 91; *need*, 95; *transformation*,
 148
lava, *energy*, 117
law, *balance*, 65
leap, *choice*, 115
learning, *intellect*, 119
leaving, *loss*, 41
lecture, *communication*, 88
leech, *risk*, 70; *stress*, 71
leg, *body*, 67
legal, *balance*, 65
leprechaun, *magic*, 169
letter, *communication*, 88
liar, *communication*, 88
library, *communication*, 88; *intellect*,
 119
life, *faith*, 142; *transformation*, 148
lifeguard, *vulnerability*, 44
light, *intellect*, 119; *intuition*, 168
lighthouse, *intellect*, 119; *intuition*, 168
lightning, *energy*, 117
limp, *body*, 66; *risk*, 70; *self-esteem*,
 42
lion, *emotion*, 37; *sex*, 97
lipstick, *sex*, 97; *self-esteem*, 42;
 vulnerability, 44
liquid, *water*, 151
liquor, *risk*, 70
listening, *body*, 66; *inspiration*, 145;
 intuition, 168
liver, *body*, 66
lizard, *emotion*, 37; *magic*, 169
lock, *communication*, 88; *control*, 33
locomotive, *energy*, 117
locust, *stress*, 71
loneliness, 92
loss, 41
love, 94
lover, *love*, 94; *sex*, 97
luggage, *emotion*, 37
lust, *sex*, 97

machine, *energy*, 117
magazine, *communication*, 88
magic, 169
magician, *magic*, 169
mail, *communication*, 88
mansion, *body*, 66; *wealth*, 122
manure, *emotion*, 37; *stress*, 71
map, *communication*, 88; *intuition*,
 168
market, *wealth*, 122
marriage, *love*, 94

mascara, *sex*, 97; *self-esteem*, 42;
 vulnerability, 44
mask, *self-esteem*, 42; *vulnerability*, 44
masturbation, *sex*, 97
matador, *risk*, 70; *stress*, 71; *vulnerability*,
 44
mate, *friendship*, 91; *love*, 94; *need*, 95;
 sex, 97
mathematics, *choice*, 115; *intellect*, 119;
 self-esteem, 42
maze, *communication*, 88
meadow, *faith*, 142; *intuition*, 168
measurement, *choice*, 115; *intellect*, 119;
 self-esteem, 42
measurement, *balance*, 65
medal, *vulnerability*, 44
medicine, *body*, 66; *stress*, 71
meditation, *inspiration*, 145; *stress*, 71
melt, *self-esteem*, 42
menopause, *body*, 66; *transformation*, 148
menstruation, *body*, 66
message, *intuition*, 168
messenger, *communication*, 88
metal, *energy*, 117; *magic*, 169
microscope, *intellect*, 119; *intuition*, 168;
 vulnerability, 44
minister, *sacredness*, 147
miracle, *faith*, 142; *intuition*, 168; *magic*,
 169; *sacredness*, 147
mirage, *vulnerability*, 44
mirror, *self-esteem*, 42
miscarriage, *risk*, 70; *transformation*, 148
miser, *wealth*, 122
misery, *loneliness*, 92; *loss*, 41; *need*, 95;
 risk, 70
misplace, *loss*, 41
missing, *loss*, 41; *self-esteem*, 42;
 vulnerability, 44
mist, *intuition*, 168; *opportunity*, 121;
 transformation, 148
monastery, *sacredness*, 147
money, *wealth*, 122
monk, *sacredness*, 147
monkey, *work*, 125
monster, *magic*, 169; *risk*, 70
mood, *emotion*, 37
moon, *faith*, 142; *inspiration*, 145;
 intuition, 168
moose, *emotion*, 37; *work*, 125
mortgage, *wealth*, 122
mortuary, *transformation*, 148
mosque, *sacredness*, 147
mosquito, *risk*, 70; *stress*, 71
mother, *love*, 94; *need*, 95
motor, *energy*, 117

plague, *body,* 66; *risk,* 70; *stress,* 71;
  vulnerability, 44
plane, *inspiration,* 145; *opportunity,* 121
plants, *faith,* 142; *intuition,* 168;
  opportunity, 121
platinum, *wealth,* 122
playground, *innocence,* 143; *joy,* 68
playing, *innocence,* 143; *joy,* 68
pleasure, *joy,* 68
poetry, *inspiration,* 145
poison, *risk,* 70
police, *communication,* 88; *control,* 33;
  criticism, 36
poll, *communication,* 88
pollution, *risk,* 70
pond, *water,* 151
pool, *water,* 151
pope, *sacredness,* 147
pornography, *sex,* 97
porpoise, *water,* 151
port, *vulnerability,* 44
poverty, *wealth,* 122
powerlessness, *need,* 95
prayer, *faith,* 142; *intuition,* 168;
  sacredness, 147
preacher, *sacredness,* 147
precognition, *clairvoyance,* 166
prediction, *clairvoyance,* 166
pregnancy, *transformation,* 148
prejudice, *anger,* 63; *emotion,* 37; *risk,* 70;
  self-esteem, 42
premonition, *clairvoyance,* 166
prescription, *body,* 66; *stress,* 71
president, *communication,* 88; *control,* 33;
  criticism, 36
priest, *sacredness,* 147
print, *communication,* 88
prison, *control,* 33; *risk,* 70; *vulnerability,*
  44
prisoner, *control,* 33; *risk,* 70;
  vulnerability, 44
prize, *vulnerability,* 44
profanity, *risk,* 70; *stress,* 71
professor, *intellect,* 119
propeller, *energy,* 117
prophet, *intuition,* 168
prophylactic, *risk,* 70; *sex,* 97
prostitution, *sex,* 97
protection, *vulnerability,* 44
proverb, *intuition,* 168
psychic, *clairvoyance,* 166
puddle, *water,* 151
puppy, *friendship,* 91; *innocence,* 143
purgatory, *magic,* 169; *risk,* 70
purse, *wealth,* 122

pursuit, *choice,* 115; *control,* 33; *need,* 95;
  self-esteem, 44; *stress,* 71; *vulnerability,*
  44
puzzle, *communication,* 88
pyramid, *intuition,* 168; *magic,* 169

quarrel, *anger,* 63; *communication,* 88;
  risk, 70
queen, *control,* 33; *criticism,* 36
quicksand, *risk,* 70; *stress,* 71;
  vulnerability, 44
quilt, *communication,* 88; *vulnerability,* 44

rabbi, *sacredness,* 147
rabbit, *emotion,* 37; *work,* 125
race, *risk,* 70; *vulnerability,* 44
racism, *anger,* 63; *emotion,* 37; *risk,* 70;
  self-esteem, 44
radar, *choice,* 115; *clairvoyance,* 166;
  intuition, 168
radiance, *love,* 94
radiation, *risk,* 70; *stress,* 71; *vulnerability,*
  44
radio, *communication,* 88
railroad, *energy,* 117; *communication,* 88
rain, *water,* 151
rainbow, *inspiration,* 145; *intuition,* 168;
  love, 94
rape, *anger,* 63; *risk,* 70; *vulnerability,* 44
rat, *emotion,* 37
raven, *inspiration,* 145; *magic,* 169
razor, *intellect,* 119; *risk,* 70
recuperate, *balance,* 65; *body,* 66; *joy,*
  68
red, *anger,* 63; *emotion,* 37; *energy,* 117;
  sex, 97
reflection, *self-esteem,* 42
refuge, *vulnerability,* 44
religion, *sacredness,* 147
remodeling, *body,* 66; *friendship,* 91;
  opportunity, 121; *self-esteem,* 42;
  transformation, 148; *work,* 125
reptile, *emotion,* 37; *magic,* 169
rescue, *criticism,* 36; *stress,* 71
resentment, *anger,* 63
resort, *risk,* 70
revenge, *anger,* 63; *emotion,* 37; *risk,* 70
rich, *wealth,* 122
ridicule, *criticism,* 36
risk, 70
river, *water,* 151
road, *choice,* 115; *intuition,* 168
robbery, *risk,* 70
robot, *loneliness,* 92; *stress,* 70;
  vulnerability, 44

rock, *energy,* 117; *stress,* 71
rocket, *energy,* 117; *inspiration,* 145;
    opportunity, 121
rodent, *emotion,* 37
romance, *love,* 94
roof, *vulnerability,* 44
room, *body,* 66
roommate, *friendship,* 91
rope, *need,* 95
rose, *innocence,* 143; *love,* 94
rowing, *stress,* 71; *work,* 125
ruby, *wealth,* 122
running, *need,* 95; *risk,* 70; *vulnerability,*
    44
rust, *transformation,* 148

sack, *choice,* 115; *emotion,* 37;
    vulnerability, 44
sacredness, 147
sadness, *loneliness,* 92; *loss,* 41; *need,* 95
saint, *sacredness,* 147
salary, *wealth,* 122
saloon, *risk,* 70
sanctuary, *sacredness,* 147; *vulnerability,*
    44
sarcasm, *criticism,* 36
Satan, *magic,* 169; *risk,* 70
scale, *balance,* 65
scalpel, *intellect,* 119; *risk,* 70
scar, *body,* 66; *risk,* 70; *vulnerability,* 44
scholar, *intellect,* 119
school, *communication,* 88; *intellect,*
    119
science, *intellect,* 119
scorpion, *risk,* 70
scream, *risk,* 70
sculpture, *choice,* 115; *inspiration,* 145
sea, *water,* 151
seance, *clairvoyance,* 166; *magic,* 169
searching, *inspiration,* 145; *intuition,*
    168
seduction, *sex,* 97
seed, *innocence,* 143; *transformation,*
    148
seizure, *body,* 66; *risk,* 70
self-esteem, 42
selfishness, *loneliness,* 92
selling, *wealth,* 122
semen, *body,* 66; *sex,* 97
seminar, *communication,* 88; *intellect,*
    119
sensual, *love,* 94; *sex,* 97
separate, *loss,* 41; *need,* 95
serpent, *emotion,* 37; *magic,* 169
sever, *loss,* 41; *need,* 95; *stress,* 71

sewing, *work,* 125
sex, 97
shadow, *control,* 33; *vulnerability,* 44
shaman, *magic,* 169
shame, *emotion,* 37
shark, *emotion,* 37; *risk,* 70
sharp, *intellect,* 119
sheep, *emotion,* 37; *work,* 125
shell, *vulnerability,* 44
shelter, *vulnerability,* 44
shepherd, *vulnerability,* 44
shield, *vulnerability,* 44
ship, *emotion,* 37; *intuition,* 168;
    loneliness, 92; *stress,* 71
shopping, *wealth,* 122
shout, *risk,* 70
shovel, *work,* 125
shower, *choice,* 115; *emotion,* 37;
    friendship, 91; *need,* 95; *transformation,*
    148
shrink, *self-esteem,* 42
shrivel, *self-esteem,* 42
shyness, *loneliness,* 92
sick, *risk,* 70
sickness, *body,* 66; *risk,* 70; *stress,* 71;
    vulnerability, 44
silver, *wealth,* 122
sinking, *loss,* 41; *risk,* 70; *stress,* 71;
    vulnerability, 44
siren, *risk,* 70
skeleton, *body,* 66; *risk,* 70
skin, *body,* 66; *vulnerability,* 44
skunk, *emotion,* 37; *work,* 125
sky, *faith,* 142; *inspiration,* 145; *intuition,*
    168
small, *self-esteem,* 42
smell, *risk,* 70
smoke, *risk,* 70; *stress,* 71; *vulnerability,* 44
smother, *anger,* 63; *balance,* 65; *body,* 66;
    control, 33; *criticism,* 36; *need,* 95; *risk,*
    70; *self-esteem,* 42; *stress,* 71;
    vulnerability, 44
snail, *emotion,* 37; *work,* 125
snake, *emotion,* 37; *magic,* 169
snow, *water,* 151
soap, *choice,* 115; *emotion,* 37; *friendship,*
    91; *need,* 95; *transformation,* 148
soaring, *inspiration,* 145
soil, *transformation,* 148
sorcery, *magic,* 169
sorrow, *loneliness,* 92; *loss,* 41; *need,*
    95
sparrow, *inspiration,* 145
spear, *magic,* 169
speech, *communication,* 88

ABOUT THE AUTHOR

Nicholas E. Heyneman, Ph.D., is a clinical psychologist, university professor, and founder of Persistence of Memory, Inc., a company devoted to personal empowerment through technology. He has published numerous professional articles and software and maintains an active private practice. Dr. Heyneman may be contacted at:

Nicholas E. Heyneman, Ph.D.
775 Yellowstone Avenue
Suite 172
Pocatello, Idaho 83201
208-234-7740
208-234-7731 (fax)
neh@srv.net